Confronting the Bull Shark

Confronting the Bull Shark

Identifying and Preparing for Catastrophic

Organizational Events

Edward Barr

BEP

BUSINESS EXPERT PRESS

Leader in applied, concise business books

Confronting the Bull Shark:
Identifying and Preparing for Catastrophic Organizational Events

Copyright © Business Expert Press, LLC, 2025

Cover design by Charlene Kronstedt

Interior design by Exeter Premedia Services Private Ltd., Chennai, India

First published in 2025 by
Business Expert Press, LLC
222 East 46th Street, New York, NY 10017
www.businessexpertpress.com

ISBN-13: 978-1-63742-750-7 (paperback)
ISBN-13: 978-1-63742-751-4 (ebook)

Business Expert Press Human Resource Management and Organizational
Behavior Collection

First edition: 2025

10 9 8 7 6 5 4 3 2 1

Description

Every organization will experience a crisis. Some will be mild; others will be severe. All will experience the unexpected. Few will experience the TOTALLY UNEXPECTED NEGATIVE EVENTS—the BULL SHARK events. These events can only be dreamed of—in a nightmare. They arise out of some deep part of an organization that believes it has things under control, much as Bull Sharks arise out of completely unexpected freshwater river to thrash and kill its prey.

Too many organizations never plan for any kind of crisis. They don't identify their vulnerabilities, typically obvious ones. A Bull Shark event is different, it's insidious. It lies deep beneath the surface, defying imagination and totally unexpected, causing chaos and havoc, threatening the life of the organization that it attacks.

However, even a Bull Shark event can be imagined. But it takes a commitment to freeing people's imaginations and then planning for these totally unlikely events. This handbook offers the insights that will help organizations go beyond the obvious to the events that make no sense when they happen and disrupt organizations to the core, the Bull Shark events. It does this with examples of Bull Shark events, techniques to unearth your potential Bull Sharks, and techniques to deal with them when they arise. **Read this book so you will know how to handle even the worst crises.**

Contents

Preface

Sharks have been swimming the oceans unchallenged for thousands of years; chances are, the species that roam corporate waters will prove just as hardy.

—*Eric Gelman, Actor*

Suppose you live in Pittsburgh, Pennsylvania, or St. Louis, Missouri, or Cincinnati, Ohio, or even New York, New York State. You'd have great rivers to recreate on. You might have a canoe, or a speed boat, or a houseboat, or even a cabin cruiser. You might enjoy a nice swim on a hot summer day in one of these majestic rivers—the Allegheny, the Ohio, the Monongahela, the Mississippi, the Hudson. As you float face up on the river and watch birds soaring above you while you listen to the laughter and play of the children splashing nearby, the last thing you'd expect would be the head butt of a bull shark just before it attacks you!

You might know that bull sharks are among the most dangerous sharks in the world. They are aggressive and tend to hunt in waters where people swim. Bull sharks live throughout the world, and they've been known to swim up freshwater rivers, up to 700 miles from the ocean. They are one of the few species of shark able to live in both salt water and freshwater rivers.

Do bull sharks often attack people in the rivers of North America? Not really. But, it can happen. Do they visit Pennsylvania, Missouri, or Ohio? Probably not. Do you plan around this eventuality when you go for a swim in the local river? Not really. If someone asked you if a bull shark attack could happen, you'd probably dismiss the question or laugh it off. But, it can happen and has happened in the rivers in Australia and India. It's not likely, but you wouldn't want to be on the receiving end of a bull shark attack.

As an organization, you do not want to be struck with a crisis for which you are completely unprepared, a Bull Shark event. How this unforeseen crisis is handled will affect the future of your organization.

In the midst of this crisis, without preparedness, no one will know what to do when the sh*t hits the fan. We read about Black Swans and Gray Rhinos. But, no one tells us to think about the highly unlikely, the game changers, the TOTALLY UNEXPECTED, the Bull Sharks. This book will give you examples of crises that no one anticipated and help you understand what might have been done to anticipate and deal with them for positive outcomes, not avoid them, but respond to them immediately and fluidly.

You will see what goes wrong when Bull Sharks attack. Without time to think, people make bad decisions. These decisions can result in broken relationships, lost reputation, firings, money losses, even physical damage. Worse yet, the Bull Shark may resurface and attack again. In any event, without some thought focused on Bull Shark attacks, leaders may appear weak, disoriented, and out of control. The board may step in, relieve the CEO and executive team to minimize the damage, and work to protect the brand. It's not a pretty situation.

I have experienced crises in past jobs. I have had to understand what happened, why it happened, and what we were going to do about it. This differentiates me and this book from others who have written about crisis and crisis management but have never experienced it. When you are in the heat of a crisis, near panic, confused, running around trying to fix things, and totally disrupted, you feel the problem and you are not just reading about it. For that reason, if you can identify your vulnerabilities, expect them to happen, have plans in place to deal with them, and have structures that make your response smooth and efficient, you will mitigate some of the pressures, especially when the Bull Shark attacks. If you flail and panic, you will make mistakes that exacerbate the problems, and you may never recover from the crisis.

Acknowledgments

I wish to thank Scott Eisenberg and BEP for believing in this book, Michael Edmondson for his editing suggestions, Caleb Sun for his illustrations, and Holly Welty-Barr without whom nothing positive could have been achieved in my life, as well as my sons and daughters who give me reasons to carry on.

Introduction

A Black Swan is an unpredictable event. A Gray Rhino is a highly probable, high impact but neglected threat. What I offer here is a useable formula for dealing, not just with both, but with the crisis you would never have dreamed would happen, the Bull Shark attack.

With all respect to Nassim Nicholas Taleb, author of the bestselling book, *The Black Swan—The Impact of the Highly Improbable*, the Bull Shark takes his ideas a step farther as I relate the real-life stories of totally negative and totally unexpected crises that I faced. Taleb wrote a book of over 400 pages. You can carry this guidebook, *Confronting the Bull Shark*, with you and easily reference what you need to know when you need to know it. This is a book about practice: how to think about Bull Sharks; how to plan for them; what to do when one strikes; how to manage your life in its aftermath. This is a book you can share with your staff and colleagues. This is a book that will make you start thinking about, not just the highly improbable events, but those that lie outside of conventional thinking.

My 25-year career in marketing and public relations exposed me to several unique crises, a few of which I will discuss in this primer. I can say, from first-hand experience, that nothing compares to the fear, anxiety, confusion, and discomfort of being in the middle of a Bull Shark crisis. Cortisol flows. Stress is tangible. The media is in your face. Your several critical audiences (the board, your customers, your vendors, and others) demand to know what's happening; they demand accountability, immediately. Emotions run high. Thinking is muddled. Voices rise in anger and threat. Blame is explicit and implicit. Careers are threatened. Decisions, wise and foolish, stick to participants forever. Yes, there is nothing like a crisis to separate the sheep from the goats, those who come out smelling good, their reputations intact, and those who come out smelling sickly, their reputations frayed.

I have taught crisis response and planning and have worked with corporations as a consultant to help them unearth their vulnerabilities and peer into the depths of the waters to see if any Bull Sharks lurk there. I can tell you that almost every company will experience a crisis. But, none of that has to happen in the extreme. All it takes is preparation and a little off-the-wall thinking, brainstorming vulnerabilities, having a long, honest, and creative session about what could potentially cripple your organization.

How does one prepare for this kind of crisis, the Bull Shark event, or any crisis, that which, by its very definition, excludes preparation? You will learn the answer to that question in this little book. I will give you simple, easy-to-follow steps to prepare you for the unexpected, the totally unexpected—the Bull Shark. Even if you do not predict the exact event, you will have come close, and your plan can easily be tweaked to deal with any event.

What Exactly Is a Bull Shark?

It is a very frightening creature, one that is totally unexpected. Listen to this description of a bull shark, courtesy of the National Wildlife Federation and their website (by way of Animal Diversity Web, University of Michigan Museum of Zoology, Florida Museum of Natural History, National Geographic, The IUCN Red List of Threatened Species).

THIS MAY BE MORE THAN YOU EVER WANTED TO KNOW ABOUT SHARKS!

"Bull sharks are distinguished from other sharks by their body's high width-to-length ratio, giving them a stout appearance. Like many fish, bull sharks exhibit countershading, or dark coloration on top and light coloration on the underbelly. This helps the animals blend into their surroundings—from above, its dark back blends into the murky water below. But from below, its white belly blends into the sunlit waters above. Male bull sharks grow to about 7 feet (2.1 meters) in length, and females grow to 11 feet (3.3 meters) or more. Adults usually weigh between 200 and 500 pounds (91 to 227 kilograms)."

"Bull sharks are found in coastal waters all over the world. In the United States, they are found off the East Coast and in the Gulf of Mexico. **Unlike most sharks, bull sharks can survive in freshwater for long periods of time. They have even been found in the Mississippi and Amazon Rivers (my bolding).** They prefer shallow coastal water, which means they can often come into contact with humans. Bull sharks are often considered to be the most dangerous sharks to humans because of their aggressive tendencies and ability to migrate up rivers. However, shark attacks are extremely rare. In a typical year, fewer than 20 people die by shark attack, but more than 20 million sharks die in relation to the fishing industry."

"The bull shark is not a picky eater. The sharks eat mostly fish, but can also eat other shark species, marine mammals, birds, and turtles. Although rare, bull sharks have also been recorded eating other bull sharks. Adult sharks tend to hunt by themselves."

"Bull sharks rarely come together, except to mate. Offsprings are usually born in the spring or summer, except in warm climates where young ones may be born year-round. Bull sharks usually live for 12 to 16 years, but one bull shark in captivity was recorded living up to 30 years old."

"These fish are listed as near-threatened. Because of their coastal distribution, bull sharks are more at risk from pollution and habitat degradation than other species. They are intentionally caught for their fins, liver oil, and skin, and are sometimes caught unintentionally as well. In addition, some bull sharks are caught for display in aquariums."

"Bull sharks have special glands and kidney functions to help their bodies retain salt while in freshwater."

www.nwf.org/en/Educational-Resources/Wildlife-Guide/Fish/Bull-Shark#:~:text=Bull%20sharks%20are%20distinguished%20from,light%20coloration%20on%20the%20underbelly

How Terrible Is a Real Bull Shark Event?

This book would be less effective without a story about a real Bull Shark attack and the unexpected nature of its actions involving a young girl in Australia. The following article has been copied from the magazine, *Business Insider*, about a Bull Shark attack on February 6, 2023:

A 16-year-old girl killed in a shark attack was swimming in a river, not the ocean. Bull sharks—considered by some experts the most dangerous—are the rare species that swim in fresh water.

- A teen in Perth was killed by a shark after jumping in a river to swim with dolphins, officials said.
- Officials believe it was a bull shark, a species known for its aggressiveness and ability to swim in freshwater.
- Bull sharks have been documented swimming up the Mississippi River as far as Illinois.

Though shark attacks are rare, they most commonly happen in the ocean, off the coast of beach destinations like Florida. But when a 16-year-old girl in Australia was killed in a shark attack on a Saturday, she wasn't swimming in the ocean.

Stella Berry was with friends riding jet skis in the Swan River, located in the city of Perth in Western Australia, when her friends said she decided to jump in the water to swim with dolphins that had been seen nearby. Her friends witnessed the attack, with Australian authorities calling it an "extremely traumatic" incident for everyone involved.

Don Punch, the Australian fisheries minister, said on Sunday it was too early to confirm the species of the shark involved, but said that it was believed to be a bull shark.

"We do know that bull sharks, particularly, do enter estuaries and freshwater river systems, so it is likely that may be the case," Punch told the Australian outlet ABC News.

Bull sharks are considered by many experts to be the most dangerous sharks in the world. They are found in waters around the globe and prefer to hunt in shallow, coastal areas—where people also tend to swim—during the day and night. Bull sharks can grow to be anywhere from 7 to 11 feet in length or more, weighing between 200 and 500 pounds, and are known for their aggressive nature—which is also where their name comes from.

Unlike most species of sharks, bull sharks can also swim in freshwater for extended periods of time, hence the reason they are known to enter and swim up estuaries. A study published in 2021 found two bull sharks even swam up the Mississippi River as far north as Illinois on separate trips in 1937 and 1995.

The study said the "rare appearance" of bull sharks in rivers has been reported on five continents. The authors said the "physiological adaptations" that allow the sharks to swim in freshwater, in addition to fossil records, indicate that bull sharks have long entered freshwater ecosystems.

Still, although you are more likely to encounter a bull shark in a river than another species, attacks remain uncommon.

Punch told ABC that the last deadly bull shark attack in Perth's Swan River occurred 100 years ago, in 1923.

"There's only been six recorded historical attacks in the river, and this would make it seven," he added.

The recent deadly attack has sparked some calls for additional research into bull sharks in the river, with Johan Gustafson, a marine ecologist with Griffith University, telling Perth radio station 6PR that tagging the fish would help researchers better understand them.

"Believe it or not we still don't know a large amount about them—we know broad movements and broad-scale behaviors of bull sharks but not the fine details—I think it's a wonderful idea," Gustafson told the station.

In 2022, there were 57 unprovoked shark attacks on humans worldwide, according to the Florida Museum of Natural History's International Shark Attack File. The United States leads the world in shark attacks, with 41 recorded last year, while Australia came in second with 9.

Bull sharks, great white sharks, and tiger sharks are the most common species to be involved in an attack.

www.businessinsider.com/teen-killed-shark-attack-river-bull-sharks-often-swim-freshwater-2023-2

PART 1

Bull Shark Events

CHAPTER 1

Losing a Fetus

... you probably spend more time in planning and training and designing for things to go wrong, and how you cope with them, than you do for things to go right.

—Alan Shepard, former Astronaut

Hospitals occasionally lose babies to kidnapping, doctors suffer malpractice, and surgeons are infected with COVID and AIDS. Banks overextend themselves, have employees who commit fraud, and others who embezzle. Universities have cheating scandals, free speech issues, and suicides. Crises come in all shapes and sizes to organizations of all shapes and sizes. And, each organization has weak spots. This is a book about identifying YOUR WEAK SPOTS, yes, but also about encounters with potential Bull Sharks, events no one could have ever imagined, ever.

You will see, as you read this book, that you must set aside some uninterrupted time to brainstorm potential crises, absolutely, but even more important is to brainstorm Bull Shark crises. Make this a creative, brainstorming session. Anything goes. Any possible vulnerability is brought forward. Crazy. Absurd. Unimaginable. Get your best creative minds together. Meet off-site. Forget an agenda. You have only one responsibility: imagine anything that might possibly happen to your organization, anything. Try your best to imagine the Bull Sharks, the events that seem totally ridiculous. Hire a facilitator, someone who's completely objective. Someone to rein in the naysayers and keep the juices flowing. Controlling naysayers is very important; they shut down dialogue and creativity.

Look at the areas of obvious concern. Do you have buildings with potentially weak structures? Might your CEO have sexist proclivities? Is there a possibility that someone might come to your place of business with an assault rifle intent on harming people?

For this identifying of vulnerabilities to work, you need to stretch your imagination to include not just "copycat" events, such as angry former employees bent on harming managers and staff with weapons, but unthinkable events, the Bull Sharks, such as vending machines falling on customers (don't laugh, it has happened). Or, if you own a restaurant chain, you might consider the possibility of a rat falling from the ceiling and dropping onto a customer's table (it happened in Pittsburgh). Anything can happen. In fact, I was involved in a situation that no one could have anticipated without some serious brainstorming; it was a real Bull Shark event.

A Bull Shark Crisis Story—"We Lost a Fetus!"

I once worked at a hospital that lost the fetus of a pregnant woman. Yep, you heard that right. How did that happen? I'll explain. But, first, think about the impossibility of this happening. With a true brainstorming session on vulnerabilities, the possibility may have surfaced, and we would have been better prepared. Alas, we had no brainstorming session, and the Bull Shark never did surface ... until it did.

I was called to the CEO's office on a Monday morning and was told that the hospital had lost a human fetus a week before. A woman with a few other children had come to the hospital and delivered a stillborn baby. She was asked if she wanted the hospital to dispose of the fetus or if she wanted to engage a mortician. Disposing of the fetus by the hospital would have meant incinerating it on site. The woman said she would handle the arrangements. Then, she was discharged, in keeping with the short length of stay mandated by insurance companies.

When the mortician hired by the woman came to collect the fetus a few days later, it could not be found. The pathology staff, security, and others searched for days but could not locate the small fetus. They looked everywhere, in the garbage, in labs, in pathology, everywhere, but to no avail. That's when I was called in, the PR Director, because the CEO could now see a major problem coming over the hill, that is, media attention and a lawsuit.

I asked the CEO if the woman whose baby we lost knew what was happening and was told that she did. I asked the CEO what the hospital was doing to assuage the woman. The CEO said that she had been advised by the Corporate Counsel not to continue to engage with the mother, no phone calls and no messages. I said that I thought it was a very bad idea and that one day the woman would appear on TV in her lawyer's office, crying and saying, "They lost my baby." The CEO dismissed this saying that if we talked to the woman anything we said could be part of a lawsuit. To which I replied, "We are going to be sued anyway." But, she preferred the counsel of our lawyers.

I felt that we had a real image problem on our hands, that we couldn't win, regardless of what might happen. I saw the issue as "Madonna and Child," despite the fact that the CEO and Legal Counsel told me some of the bad things the woman had been known to have done in her past. To me, she could have been any kind of horrible person, an ax murderer, but we still lost a mother's child. The media would see it that way and the public, especially mothers, would see it that way. We couldn't win and we certainly wouldn't benefit from name-calling.

While tension rose at the hospital as workers frantically searched for the fetus, a news item appeared in the local newspaper that the Coroner's Office had received a fetus from a central laundry that served three hospitals in the city, ours included, and a university hospital that engaged in research involving monkeys. The coroner, a well-known personality, acclaimed to the media that the laundry service had sent him a "monkey fetus." That didn't go unnoticed by our pathologist who had autopsied the fetus (as required by law).

It's important to know that when the coroner, a doctor, said the fetus they received was a monkey, he effectively put his reputation on the line. It started to look like our war was opening on another front, not just with the mother but also with the coroner.

"They Lost My Baby"

In the meantime, we knew the fetus was missing because the mortician who came for the body could not find it in the hospital morgue and the staff couldn't produce it. While we continued to search for the fetus, the woman, as I had predicted, appeared on the nightly TV news in her lawyer's office, crying, and saying, "They lost my baby." For me, it was an "I-told-you-so" moment. And now, because there wasn't much happening in the media, the news media was fully interested in the story, all of the local news media—newspapers, TV stations, and radio stations. At the same time, the pathologist who had autopsied the baby went to the Coroner's Office, examined the fetus, and determined, by the suture marks, that it was the baby he had autopsied and that we had lost.

Why did he autopsy the baby? At the time, state law mandated that after a certain period of gestation and a certain size and weight, even babies who had expired had to be autopsied.

"Monkey Business at Mercy"

Now, the media jumped into the story with both feet (it was a slow news week, as it happened). One newspaper ran the headline on the front page after it got wind of the coroner's part in the drama and our pathologist's role, "Monkey Business at Mercy." The mother was interviewed by all TV stations and other media (not social media at the time). We were definitely in a tight, and hot, spot. On top of that, the Corporate Counsel continued to advise the CEO, "Don't say anything," while I begged the CEO to stand before the media, apologize, empathize (the CEO was a woman), sympathize, and above all open communication with the mother.

Is It a Monkey Fetus or a Human Fetus?

You may think that this could have been easily resolved by having someone declare it either simian or human. But, it wasn't that simple. The fetus had been washed and dried in high temperatures at the central laundry and had become partially dismembered.

By now, the pathologist had convinced the CEO that the fetus at the Coroner's Office was the one we lost. The CEO asked the coroner to send the fetus to a famous women's hospital in the city. He did and, we later learned, sent it in a jar labeled "Monkey Fetus." The famous women's hospital said it was a monkey. Then we asked to have it sent to a research center at a well-known university in the city. The same thing happened. Their noted anthropologist said it was a monkey. Our pathologist who was by now out on a gag order by the CEO maintained that it was the lost fetus. He stepped out of bounds and contacted an expert at the Smithsonian in Washington, District of Columbia, a physician who asked to see the fetus. He, too, received the jar labeled "Monkey Fetus." He then concurred with the coroner and said it was a monkey fetus. Surprised at this, the pathologist contacted the doctor in the District of Columbia and asked the expert if he knew of the lost human fetus in Pittsburgh, the autopsy, and the suture marks. He didn't. He was appalled upon learning the full context. He connected with the coroner and expressed his dismay that the jar had come to him with the erroneous label.

If things weren't bad enough, the hospital did not want to antagonize the coroner since coroners rule over all wrongful deaths. Hospitals have wrongful deaths. Something like 100,000 people die from wrongful deaths and accidents, in America's hospitals every year. It's not a good idea for a hospital to piss off the coroner.

The media continued to question the parties involved and, feeling the pressure, the coroner agreed to host a joint press conference with the CEO. The room was packed. Our CEO sat next to the coroner. The two of them had agreed that the coroner would say that the hospital had done nothing wrong. He never did admit that the fetus was a human. Other news grabbed the media's attention and the event faded.

In the next month, the woman sued the hospital and received a fairly insignificant sum in an out-of-court settlement. And, as far as I know, the fetus is still at the coroner's office in a jar labeled "Monkey Fetus." At that point, the tension, stress, pressure, pain, and other negative feelings that accompany a crisis slipped away. But, it could have ruined the hospital, especially the OB/GYN practice at the hospital. It also could have gone much more smoothly if we had anticipated a crisis somewhat like the crisis we suffered. We just needed to imagine that it could happen and be prepared to deal with it; we needed to be thinking of Bull Sharks.

Post Script (PS)

After the crisis of the lost fetus quieted, the hospital continued to investigate what might have happened. This was their conclusion:

When the woman delivered the stillborn fetus, a staff person took it to pathology. As was mentioned earlier, Pennsylvania law required that any human above a certain size had to be autopsied after a questionable death. The pathologist autopsied the fetus by making incisions and closed the body with sutures. Then, what likely happened, was that another staff person took the fetus wrapped in a small blanket to the hospital morgue where it was laid in the freezer drawer WITHOUT A BODY TAG on either the fetus or the drawer handle. It is suspected that another person who needed a drawer for another body opened the drawer with the fetus, saw a small blanket, and threw it into the laundry, whereupon the laundry service, a service not owned or operated by the hospital and serving several others, took the laundry to their laundry facility and laundered it. When they discovered it, they assumed that it came from a research facility and sent it to the coroner who, when told that it came from a research facility, named it a monkey.

Again, this was a Bull Shark. It arose out of nowhere. No one predicted its eventuality. Could it have surfaced during brainstorming? We will never know. But, with the right imagination, it might have. That's the contention of this book—Bull Sharks exist and can be anticipated.

Post Post Script (PPS)

Not long after the lost fetus incident, someone brought a deer heart to the hospital (presumably a worker) and left it near the trash collection site. A worker saw it and naturally thought it was a human heart. This generated a lot of anxiety that was not abated until cardiologists examined the heart and tissue samples were examined to prove that it was not a human heart but likely that of an animal, perhaps a deer since the episode happened during Pennsylvania's Deer Season.

What Went Wrong and What Could Have Been Corrected?

"Hindsight is 20–20," as the saying goes. It's true, but every organization must review a crisis after the fact and objectively assess the positives and negatives, trying to determine what it could have done differently.

1. PREPAREDNESS. This organization had no real crisis preparedness, let alone preparation for a Bull Shark event. It needed to implement a process within the organization to allow all departments to brainstorm and anticipate wildly improbable, as well as relatively likely crisis events, to happen. For instance, it could have asked its maternity unit to identify possible troubling events. For instance, it may have surfaced a baby kidnapping. Think of this situation: a husband and wife are estranged. Yet, the wife is pregnant. She has told the husband that he will not be part of the baby's life. The husband retaliates by visiting the hospital nursery, identifies himself as the father, and takes

the child. Stranger things have happened … including the loss of a fetus. Having thought of the kidnapping possibility, the maternity unit could use the crisis planning document, created and shared by the executive group, to create a plan to avoid kidnapping and be able to act quickly on it if it happened.

2. LEGAL COUNSEL. The organization relied too heavily on the advice of legal counsel. Many lawyers make conservative decisions. It's their rule, in many ways. But here, the theme was "Madonna and Child." It was a no-win situation. The general public, especially women, was not going to side with the typically impersonal hospital/medical message.

3. TEAMWORK. Critical minds were not engaged quickly enough. The people who managed the media were not involved for over a week while the hospital searched in vain for the fetus. The pathologist was effectively kept out of the process. The message was, "You're a doctor. You helped us lose the fetus. Stay out of this." It wasn't until the news media announced that a monkey had been delivered to the coroner's office that the pathologist involved himself, without permission.

4. DIALOGUE. Because it was thinking like a business and through a legal lens, the organization cut dialogue with the birth mother and the media. It amounted to a gag order. It amounted to a lack of emotional intelligence. It looked like fear and guilt.

5. DELAY. The organization kept up a futile attempt to find the fetus, while the pathologist, who had gone to the coroner's office and examined the supposed monkey fetus, insisted that the fetus was at the coroner's office. If it hadn't been tragic, it would have been comical. Finally, after getting its butt kicked for a week by the media, the Chairman of the Board of the hospital interceded and called a meeting of the CEO, Legal Counsel, VP for Administration, and Director of Corporate Communication (a meeting that should have been called immediately). At a high-end private club to which the Chairman belonged, the group decided to approach the coroner and settle the matter of the fetus.

6. EMPATHY. The organization lacked emotional intelligence. It didn't empathize with the woman or her family. It turned away from her on advice from legal counsel. It turned cold and callous.

7. AFTER-ACTION REPORT. The organization did not conduct a full-scale and objective review of the Bull Shark event. It learned a valuable lesson about crisis management but did not turn that learning into a process.

Discussion Questions

1. Are you vulnerable? If so in what ways?

2. Do you have interactions with a large, diverse staff, such as in a hospital, university, mall, restaurant, airline?

3. Do you provide a service?

4. Does your organization have set procedures to prevent breakdowns. Do you regularly review these procedures?

5. How does communication occur in your workplace?

6. How could this event have been avoided?

7. How will this organization recover from this event?

8. Is your organization vulnerable to this kind of crisis?

CHAPTER 2

Falling Buildings

Well, I'm not excusing the fact that planning and preparedness was not where it should be. We've known for 20 years about this hurricane, this possibility of this kind of hurricane.
—Michael Chertoff, former Secretary of U.S. Department of Homeland Security on Hurricane Katrina

Most organizations don't think about a potential crisis, or they just ignore the possibility of it happening. When "Sh*t Happens" then, they are caught completely off guard. This is especially true of Bull Shark events. Perhaps something happens at two in the morning when all the executives are snoring in bed. Maybe they're in another city or country. They get a frantic call that awakens them, and they bolt upright in their pajamas, wide-eyed and panicky. They usually call the person in the organization they trust the most to see what she or he knows about the situation. They likely begin a telephone tree (and might already have one). What they don't have is a crisis team. When the Bull Shark strikes, the CEO frantically decides whom they should bring into the office or on a Zoom call and they agree to meet. What happens next is anyone's guess. But, it doesn't have to be.

You've Got to Respond Quickly

Do yourself a favor. Identify a crisis team TODAY. Keep the team SMALL. Who should belong? The CEO, the COO, the corporate counsel, the chief medical officer (CMO), and the security chief. Forget the board chair or other board members. Keep them informed but keep them away from the day-to-day, just as you should every day. The team I have just suggested will make the big and broad decisions, the final decisions, legal decisions, security decisions, operational decisions, and media decisions. Too many chefs spoil the broth. An unwieldy group can make quick decisions and quick responses impossible.

A Bull Shark Crisis Story—"The Building's Falling!"

As the Director of PR at a very large employer, one of the largest in the city, I once received a call at 6 a.m. that an entire wing, all eight stories of a building housing hundreds of people, was falling into a demolition/construction site adjacent to it and on a hillside about 100 feet above. It was truly a Bull Shark event.

This particular building, the "E Wing," was relatively new and sat above a site where a century-old building had been demolished to make way for a 12-story tower. Staff in the "E Wing" had seen cracks in the plaster where they swore that they had not seen cracks before and some staff said they heard "cracking" noises. Panic was beginning to build.

This organization had no formal crisis team (not even an informal one), but the CEO had been alerted, and my boss, a VP of Operations, had notified the CEO and I was told to meet them at the construction site. When I got there, more than 20 people surrounded the CEO —VPs, staff, construction workers, architects, maintenance staff, even environmental workers (aka janitors). It was a scene of bedlam, like a bunch of hyenas chewing the carcass of a kill.

The group had several recommendations, all based on their areas of expertise—evacuate the building, seal the cracks, wait to see what happens, manage the news media (what exactly do we tell them). The whole thing bordered on hysteria. There were just too many people involved (interestingly there was no lawyer present, or it would have been crazier).

"Don't Say Anything to the Media"

I was told not to comment to the media. This was a mistake, of course. It was a small town; people who worked in the building had probably already called their relatives and friends telling them their versions of what was happening. Although one should never speculate with the media, we could at least have told them, indeed we should have told them, what we knew. And, we should have done it proactively.

"Don't Tell Anyone I Told You"

As the PR guy and the direct link between the media and the organization, I felt obligated to tell the most important and responsible newsperson what I knew about the situation. He was good. He had his contacts inside the organization. He would interview many staff, anyway, for the same information if I didn't tell him. I felt this was in the best interest of the organization. I took the initiative and asked him not to attribute the comments to me and he didn't. His story in the newspaper was accurate, balanced, and fair.

In the End

When all was said and done, the building didn't fall into the construction site, but the contractors did put up some retaining beams just to stay on the side of caution. The media followed the story from the early newspaper account, which I had engineered and the damage to the organization (not a pun on purpose) and its image was minimal.

The Bottom Line

I learned through the two crises just described that Bull Sharks attack at the most inopportune times. They rise up when you're not looking, and they disable you quickly. I also learned that a crisis team is an absolute necessity, a team that is small, manageable, agile, and authoritative. Without it you have total chaos. Which leads us to the next prerequisite in crisis management, appointing the right spokesperson, coaching that person, and practicing with her or him.

What Went Wrong and What Could Have Been Corrected?

1. PREPAREDNESS. This organization had no crisis planning. None. It just didn't exist. That, of course, is a huge problem. Essentially, no one knew what to do when the event happened. It was literally like chickens running around with their heads cut off. They might have brainstormed beforehand any number of crisis scenarios had they taken the time. When you have any construction, there are always people potentially affected by it and adverse events can always occur. Would they have guessed the possible collapse of a five-story building into a construction hole? Who knows. If they were thinking, they could have predicted staff poisoning patients, explosions at nearby factories necessitating an overflow of severely wounded patients, or just about any human frailty or possibility.

2. CRISIS TEAM. There was NO crisis team and, of course, no crisis support team. When the event happened, all eyes turned to the CEO who turned his eyes to the contractors, who took over the investigation. The CEO used his natural leadership to visit the building and talk to the staff. But, organizations cannot rely on charisma, especially at a crisis onset, to make things right.

3. COORDINATION. With the rumors of a possible building collapse circulating through the organization, the need for immediate central coordination was mandatory. Picture this: five

floors of patients in rooms needed to be evacuated along with their belongings. Staff had to be managed and coordinated. Even furniture may have needed to be moved.

4. COMMUNICATION. The most essential need was timely, accurate, and honest communication. Not only was this necessary for internal audiences, but it was hypercritical for external audiences. This was especially true of the news media. The best tact when something like this happens is to partner with many different entities. Certainly, alerting the news media and not stonewalling them would best serve the organization's purposes. In the small town, news travels fast through informal channels—like nurses calling their families and patients calling their families—so the news media will learn both facts and fiction. Obviously, you want them to know and report the facts, as they have been gathered to that point. The fact that the PR person spoke to the media without the approval of the CEO speaks of the lack of trust and understanding of PR's role in a crisis. In addition, there was no form of rapid internal communication to help quell the rumors.

5. AFTER ACTION REPORT. Just like other crises, the organization did not conduct a full scale and objective review of the Bull Shark event. It had the opportunity to learn valuable lessons about crisis management, but it did not turn that learning into a process.

Discussion Questions

1. Is your organization undergoing any major construction or renovations?

2. Have you identified all areas of the organization that will be affected?

3. Have you identified key people in each area that will attend meetings on the construction plans and timeline?

4. Have you considered the impact on customers and staff of the construction activity?

5. Is there any unusual or dangerous equipment being used?

6. Could panic in this event been prevented?

7. How will an organization recover after an event like this?

8. Is your organization vulnerable to this kind of crisis?

CHAPTER 3

Nuns Play "Miami Vice"

No matter how good you are at planning, the pressure never goes away. So I don't fight it. I feed off it. I turn pressure into motivation to do my best.

—Ben Carson, former Secretary of Housing and Urban Development

When you appoint a spokesperson during a crisis, it can only be the CEO. Sorry. I don't care how inarticulate that person might feel about himself or herself. Appoint the CEO. Anyone else is NOT the final authority, especially in a Bull Shark event. COACH this person in the ways to deal with the media. Insist on it. Lots of CEOs rise to the top because of their intelligence and experience, but few have a depth of experience with the media, and even fewer have experience with the media when the Bull Sharks rise.

Practice. Videotape the CEO. Connect the CEO to the reporters so that they feel comfortable with each other and can solve problems together and not be adversaries. President Reagan famously handled the media with wit and honesty, and he survived the Iran Contra Affair with barely a scratch. If you become an adversary of the media, you can only lose. President Nixon detested the media and treated them as adversaries, and they became the adversaries that took down his presidency. Be open, honest, and accessible. Respect what the reporters are trying to do, and they will likely respect you. Give them a hard time and I promise they will make your life miserable.

Bull Shark Crisis Story—Nuns Play Miami Vice

I was called into the CEO's office yet again. Another Bull Shark had arisen. The CEO told me in confidence that the employees of the parking services of the hospital had been stealing money for several years, probably over $1 million, one parking receipt at a time. When I asked the CEO how she knew this, she said that a new worker at the garage was told about the scam and warned that he had to participate or lose his job.

I had built a pretty solid relationship with a Pulitzer Prize-winning reporter from one of the city's newspapers and had put him together with the CEO as often as possible to build their relationship. Now, I thought was a good time to have them help each other.

I was greatly concerned that the story could break as "Dumb and Naïve Nuns Lose $1 Million in Garage Rip-Off." But, the CEO told me that she had hired a team of private detectives from Miami to investigate the employee's claims. I convinced her and the VP she had put in charge of the operation to let the reporter in at that point. I saw the story unfolding as "Nuns Play Miami Vice," a different, and positive, spin. At that time, "Miami Vice" was a very popular TV crime show, starring Crocket and Tubbs (actors Don Johnson and Philip Michael Thomas), that changed the nature of TV shows because of its use of music, storytelling, and production. This could work for us, but the CEO and VP had to let the reporter have access. And, they did. They were open, honest, and accessible with him.

The hired private detectives from Miami played it like Miami Vice. They worked under cover. They videotaped the garage from the roof of an adjoining building. They used marked bills when paying for their parking. But, the coup de grace happened when they invited the parking garage employees to a "Christmas Party," where hospital security and local detectives hustled each one to a private room and confronted each with the evidence, breaking them down to rat on each other. Most gave up their accomplices quickly and the saga ended with arrests. It was sad that it had to happen, but it ended on a positive note. Imagine nuns in their black habits (they didn't wear them but the image lingered anyway) furtively hiding in darkness with video cameras and Nikon cameras!

The crisis ended well because the CEO made herself accessible and she made her lieutenant, the VP, accessible. In the end both spoke to the broader media, adding credibility to the story. What could have been a PR disaster, ruining reputations, made the nuns look like geniuses.

It also ended well because the CEO had been prepared. She knew the reporter and trusted him (that wasn't an easy accomplishment as all executives have little trust of the media). She was an articulate woman who also trusted me (too many executives devalue PR people). She was willing to take a risk by letting the reporter in on the story. That was a huge risk.

The CEO Can Make or Break a Crisis

Crisis management stories are rife with CEOs who were indecisive, fearful, and motivated by concerns unrelated to their audiences. These CEOs have avoided the media or made some pretty stupid statements. Look at the history of crisis mismanagement and you will find the Bhopal disaster, the Exxon Valdez, and a host of other crisis management failures where CEOs were indecisive, arrogant, and often just plain stupid.

Could This Crisis Have Been Anticipated?

Sadly, yes. It suggests a too-lax approach to financial management and accounting and a failure to identify vulnerabilities, especially the Bull

Sharks. Humans have inherent weaknesses that lead them to be greedy, jealous, sexist, and frail. As a result, anything can happen because of their foibles. It's in the best interest of any CEO to mandate the brainstorming of vulnerabilities to be as creative as possible, to unearth any seemingly ridiculous idea, the Bull Shark, about how the company might have a crisis on its hands.

Organizations that have the best relationships with employees, especially those at the bottom core of the business, can be made aware of weaknesses that management would be unaware of. Creating a culture of openness encourages employees to share concerns for areas of potential problems.

What Went Wrong and What Could Have Been Corrected?

1. PREPAREDNESS. The organization had experienced crises, but still did not bake crisis planning into its systems. If it had, it may have anticipated this Bull Shark, after all people have frailties and some are dishonest, dishonest enough to take advantage of a nonprofit organization. The parking garage sat immediately across the street from the CEO's office. It was something she, the other executives, and many employees looked at—or parked in—every day. Leading a very profitable nonprofit and having a fine education, the CEO was no dummy. She had the respect of her board and of many business leaders in the city. But, she like many CEOs never dreamed of the kinds of events that can happen. It is said that "an ounce of prevention is worth a pound of cure" and that sentiment fits across all organizations. Prepare. Prepare. Prepare. But, do more than that, anticipate the Bull Shark events. Let your imagination run wild. Look across the street at that parking garage. Imagine the workers skimming money. It can happen.

2. COMMUNICATION. In this instance, the CEO did a good thing; she involved PR and the media in the situation. She trusted both. This only happened because the PR person had

built trust with the CEO and the VP who had been assigned primary responsibility.

3. COORDINATION. The CEO was able to control the situation because the number of persons who had information about the fraud was limited to her, a VP of Operations, PR, legal counsel, and the chairman of the board. A crisis support team was unnecessary due to the nature of the situation and the decisions that had been made. The sting operation was effectively handled by outside contractors who were, of course, managed by the CEO and her VP.

4. AFTER ACTION REPORT. This Bull Shark event could have served as impetus to implement full-scale crisis planning, but it didn't. I'm not sure why. Perhaps because, as crises go, it was considered a success. The perpetrators were caught, the story depicted, not dumb nuns who had been taken advantage of in their naivety, but shrewd sisters who had run a Miami Vice sting and brought justice to the villains. That's what people remembered. They didn't remember that $1 million dollars had been lost to fraud because the nuns had trusted a group they had dealt with for years to manage and operate the parking garage. If anything, the event showed them that they could trust PR, not to spin the story but to show the CEO in a light that she deserved, a woman able to assume a different role and act it well.

Discussion Questions

1. Do you have a Crisis Team in place?

2. Does your organization deal with vulnerable clients?

3. If so, are the buildings that house them safe and secure?

4. Do your facilities have security cameras to monitor clients in a crisis?

5. Is your organization vulnerable to this kind of crisis?

CHAPTER 4

Doing a "Peter Pan"

Everyone has a plan until they get punched in the mouth.
—Mike Tyson, former heavyweight champion of the world

With any crisis, fast action and decision making are important; they are the province of the crisis team. But, details are critical. Security people must deal with security issues; PR must deal with communication matters; operations must keep the business running. The crisis team can't do it all. Therefore, it's important that a separate support team be ready to respond. This team must consist of RELIABLE PEOPLE. This group will manage many of the crisis DETAILS and deliver much of the crisis SUPPORT MATERIAL. Human resources (HR) belongs to this team, along with people from finance, customer relations, as well as subject matter experts and social media specialists.

Bull Shark Crisis Story—"He Did a Peter Pan Right out of This Window"

In the movie, "The Fugitive," Richard Kimble (Harrison Ford) runs away from a train derailment only to be chased by U.S. Marshal Samuel Gerard (Tommy Lee Jones). One chase scene ends at an aqueduct where Kimble jumps into an enormous waterfall and is presumed to have drowned. Standing at the top of the waterfall, Gerard says to a deputy, "Guy did a Peter Pan right here off this dam." Gerard is shocked that Kimble would choose to potentially jump to his death rather than be taken into custody. Gerard underestimated the desperation of Kimble. Failing to truly understand the desperation of a person's mental state of mind can create a Bull Shark situation.

The professionals caring for a patient in a hospital I worked for failed to properly evaluate the desperation of a patient. I was called in the middle of the night to learn that a patient jumped from a window to his death at the hospital. It was another Bull Shark event.

But He Was Predicted as a Jumper

When I arrived at the hospital, I tried to gather as much information as possible about the situation. I was told by a nurse that the deceased had been anxious and threatening to kill himself. The nurses gave him tranquilizers, powerful ones, locked the windows, and finally strapped the patient into bed. But, he somehow managed to release himself, leave his bed, and jump through the window in the room, glass and all. He landed three stories below; the fall killed him.

What made this a Bull Shark? No one imagined that he had the physical power to overcome sedatives. No one could imagine that he would remove the restraints that bound him or that he would jump through the window without opening it. Everyone was too busy doing what they normally do, going about their business, following their protocols.

I was alone with the situation with one junior administrator and expected to manage media inquiries, the first consideration. I convinced the administrator that it was best to alert the media. He was skeptical but finally relented. I then took the initiative and called the radio stations first, at 5 a.m., because I knew they would be first to report what had happened and by 12 p.m. the story could be stale. I had no crisis team or crisis support team to help.

Imagine what may have happened: the CEO gets a call about the crisis, she uses her previously created communication tools to bring her crisis team together—in person or virtually. They gather information and discuss the matter and then make decisions. Meanwhile the crisis support team has been activated and gathered. The crisis team decisions are relayed to them and they take the initiative to manage many details. All runs smoothly.

We Needed a Crisis Support Team

How could the team have helped me? First, I had no idea of the legal ramifications; legal counsel would have helped with that. I knew the policies for patient disclosure and did not release the name of the patient. But, I had no understanding of the medical implications (a CMO as part of the crisis team would have helped me on that score). Security was on the scene, but they were a little too controlling and guarded, as security tend to be. I was the lone communication person and had to generate messages for all audiences. A crisis support team would have helped to formulate a cohesive message. At this time, the hospital had no central meeting place and no telephone chain. They incorrectly assumed that they would never have the need for any of these things because what could possibly happen in a smaller community hospital. They were wrong on all counts. Fortunately, this occurred before social media, or I would have been doubly hamstrung.

In situations such as this one, every detail is critical. One person cannot manage it all. It requires a team of people who trust each other and commit to seeing the problem to its solution.

This is especially true in the Bull Shark event. A totally unexpected event had occurred, an event that no one had anticipated, and the organization was compromised. It should have imagined such a scenario and created a plan to deal with it. Plans are helpful, even when they must change. A crisis team must be in place at all times to respond to crises and it must have the people, facilities, and materials it needs to do its job well.

Team Needs

To function well, a crisis team will need:

- Team meeting rooms;
- Team members' phone numbers and other contact information;
- Equipment (video recorders, pens, pencils, TVs, radios, daily newspapers, telephones, and computers).

Refreshments for the crisis team:

- FAQs about the organization;
- Relevant statistics;
- A media room with computers, telephones, refreshments, podium, and other essentials for the media;
- And, of course, the crisis plans.

More Suicides

Unfortunately, the organization had repeated suicides. In a second situation, a patient pried open a very small window, hardly enough to fit herself through, and fell only 12 feet, but it was enough to kill her. The patient wandered into a stairwell, found the window, and exited. Suddenly, the hospital became known for its suicides, just as a building on a Pittsburgh university campus became known for its suicides. (The university finally remedied the situation by replacing all windows with small vents.)

What Went Wrong and What Could Have Been Corrected?

1. PREPAREDNESS. If you have a building, someone is likely to jump from it to their death. If the building has windows, that

doesn't mean it has to be open for someone to jump through it. Doesn't this seem like an obvious need for a crisis plan? But, you say, we have security officers and capable staff. Sorry, as the popular wisdom says, "Where there's a will there's a way." People are unendingly inventive; they will find ways to kill themselves. They will find ways to disrupt your organization. They will steal, lose a fetus, poison your well, anything. For that reason, you must stay ahead of every crisis. You must anticipate the Bull Sharks. They arrive where they're not supposed to be. At one time, a university (which I will not name) had a rash of suicides; in fact, most universities can and should anticipate suicidal teenagers. One suicide is a tragic event; several suicides is a crisis. That university should have had plans in place to effectively deal with a suicide.

2. SUPPORT. When crises occur, no one person can handle them. There are too many moving parts. But, too much support, in the sense of too many people around the situation, can confuse things. Every organization—I repeat, every organization—needs a crisis team. That group makes the big decisions. But, that small group of five or six people need others, the crisis support team, who can support the decisions made at the top. If the crisis team says they will respond to the public immediately, others need to schedule the event, contact the media, secure their parking, see that they have a room, to work from, prepare talking points for the CEO, and handle the myriad other details that the CEO could never attend to. This is especially true with Bull Shark events.

3. LEGAL. Most times you do need legal in the room. They need to address liabilities and the law, but they cannot be allowed to block communication. Every—repeat, every—organization must have communication direction, whether it be from PR or marketing. Someone in the room must understand audiences, their psychologies, their biases. They must be communicated with. They cannot be allowed to make their own conclusions; they will be in error.

4. COMMUNICATION. In this instance, the organization did a good thing despite themselves. They gave the PR person enough latitude to make his own decision. He used his experience and understanding of news cycles to soften the media response. The radio news isn't typically as detailed and questioning as the print news. He knew that and used the knowledge to make the story break at 6 a.m. and become stale by 9 p.m. Legal counsel may have said, "We don't need to tell people something they may never find out about." But, good leaders will say, "We will be open, honest, and accessible to all at any time, not hiding or obfuscating." In this writer's experience, that approach always works best, always. It's true that, "Honesty is the best policy." Just ask Exxon, Union Carbide, and certainly Johnson & Johnson.

5. AFTER ACTION REPORT. The organization had a significant change not long after (but not because of) the event. The CEO left and, in short order, most of his executive team left. As a result, no crisis team was formed, no crisis planning took place, and they settled in to attend to the daily demands of running a large organization. No one understood the great necessity of crisis planning and the ways in which ignoring it can lead to a company's demise.

Discussion Questions

1. Does your organization use outside vendors to manage any part of your business?

2. Does your organization have systems to monitor outside vendors?

3. Does your organization have policies in place regarding outside vendors?

4. Does your organization employ "mystery shoppers" to report on the customer's experience?

5. Have you had an experience like this one? If so, how did you (or an organization you know about) respond?

6. Is your organization vulnerable to this kind of crisis?

CHAPTER 5

A Physician With AIDS

Think ahead. Don't let day-to-day operations drive out planning.
—Donald Rumsfeld, former United States Secretary of Defense

Create a Plan for Each of Your Most Likely Vulnerabilities

Most organizations do the opposite of what Donald Rumsfeld said, they let day-to-day operations drive out planning, especially crisis planning. Forget about Bull Shark planning; they lack the insights and energy for ordinary crisis planning, let alone typical crises.

This planning is a laborious task, but it will help immensely in the event of a Bull Shark event. The planning begins with a discussion of vulnerabilities, the obvious situations where a crisis might occur. Then with a good facilitator on hand, the group can get crazy and surface the wildest things that could happen, the true Bull Sharks. Each plan will include many IMPORTANT DETAILS. Among those are: Logistical matters such as meeting rooms, phone numbers and other contact information, equipment (video recorders, pens, pencils, TVs, radios, daily newspapers, telephones, computers), refreshments, and so on (as mentioned in the previous chapter).

Break Out the Fire Extinguishers

I like to think of the plans as fire extinguishers behind glass cases with a little hammer attached and a message that says, "Break glass in case of emergency." First, create the plans. This will require a lot of work, but it will pay off when the sh*t hits the fan. Because you all have a copy of the plans, you will all know how to reach each other, where to convene, and ultimately what to say. You will be armed with facts and statistics to help put the crisis in context. For example, you can talk about how many meals you serve (if you have a food crisis). You can talk about how many successful operations you have conducted if you have a crisis of health care. You will be able to do the most important thing: put the crisis in context.

Know who can update this information quickly. You will know how many products you have created over the years without any problems (if you have a product recall). Keep these plans handy and be ready to implement them at a moment's notice. In fact, give each member of the crisis team a copy of each plan for the day, if it should come, when a Bull Shark attacks; the plan will be needed.

Bull Shark Crisis Story—Does Your Physician Have AIDS?

Another Bull Shark arose unexpectedly. And, again, I received a call at home asking me to go to the office. A pediatric emergency department physician had been accused, anonymously, of having AIDS (this at the height of the AIDS epidemic). This, of course, had all the earmarks of a horrifying crisis, not just for the hospital but also for the physician, a wonderful, soft-spoken, and gentle young guy of great credentials and awesome bedside manners.

What do you do when a physician who has been seeing many children every day is accused of having AIDS? If it turns out to be true and you knew about it and did nothing, you are liable, not just financially, but to the health of all children who might have become infected. Do you ignore it? No. You must act. But, it brings a host of problems—physical, emotional, organizational, and so on.

Although the AIDS epidemic was in full swing, we had not made any plans to respond to a situation where a physician might have AIDS and be treating patients, a classic Bull Shark event. Not only was our situation very complicated—the AIDS scare was palpable—but we had to confront a beloved physician and ask him if he had AIDS. To begin with, he didn't have to answer that question and we had to think seriously about how to pose the question in the first place or what to do if he refused to answer. As it turned out, he was very accommodating when approached and we were pleased to hear him say that he didn't have AIDS. However, we did ask him if we could test him for it and he readily agreed.

The situation was a "no win" for all. Asking the physician if he had AIDS was difficult. Even if he didn't have AIDS, he faced the fact that a whole organization and the city may have thought he had AIDS. It was an ugly situation that could have easily ruined his reputation. However, this situation resolved peacefully and disappeared as it had no validity. The organization saw that he tested negative, and the event ended. No one saw a reason to share any further information with anyone. Because the physician was a relative rarity, a pediatric emergency room physician, he had had contact with the media from time to time and also when he was first introduced. He handled himself well at previous times with the media and when one of the reporters heard about the accusation, he spent some time with the doctor, saw the negative AIDS test, and dropped the matter.

What Would You Do If the Physician Treating Your Child Had AIDS?

Imagine the situation and procedures if the doctor had tested positive for AIDS. This happened in another city hospital. One of their surgeons tested positive for AIDS. If it's a doctor examining your child, it's one thing. If it's someone who operated on you, it's a totally different matter. At that point, you'd have to bring all patients back for AIDS testing. Some of them would comply; some would not. No one was legally compelled to submit to AIDS testing. If any patient contracted AIDS, the organization would have a legal firestorm on its hands.

A Potential PR Nightmare

Forget the legal issues and think about the PR issues if a surgeon or pediatrician tested positive for AIDS. Years of goodwill, community relations, and solid reputation could go down the drain in that scenario. On the other hand, if the organization had unearthed the seemingly never-could-happen situation, they could have planned how to respond. They could have initialized the plan when the totally unexpected crisis occurred and brought together the facts of their otherwise solid performance. They could have done this without the panic, which typically accompanies a totally unexpected crisis.

How This Situation Should Have Been Prepared For

In the best scenario, a surgeon affected with AIDS would have unfolded like this: the surgeon self-reports to the CMO that he has been tested for AIDS and is infected. The CMO informs the CEO. The CEO calls an immediate meeting of the crisis team. The CEO and CMO go to the room designated for crisis response having summoned the legal counsel, COO, CMO, and security chief. At this meeting, the crisis team, along with the infected surgeon, examines the crisis and makes broad decisions about the pending course of action, based on these questions:

- Who will present their findings and will the infected doctor be exposed?
- How and when will they notify patients?
- When will they address the media?
- How will they inform all constituents (board members, advisers, vendors, etc.)?
- What exactly will they include in their initial statement?
- How often will they update all constituents?
- Where will they hold their briefings?
- What will they do after the initial report?
- How will they manage testing of all patients of the infected surgeon?
- Should testing be enlarged to include family member of the exposed patients?
- Should operating room personnel be tested?
- What should be budgeted for operational expenses?
- What are the security issues?
- What budget will they allocate, if any, for PR/Marketing/Operations?

The Crisis Team Engages the Crisis Support Team

Now that the broad decisions have been made, much detail work begins to operationalize the plan:

- HR provides all information on the infected surgeon.
- The marketing department prepares a draft statement for the CEO to deliver.
- The marketing department prepares a set of questions and suggested responses for the CEO when addressing various audiences.
- The PR officer arranges for a media conference by reserving a room and equipping it with appropriate technology and distributing support materials.
- Security officers are briefed on the crisis and expectations concerning security issues.

- Security arranges for parking and movement through the organization.
- Operations plans for an all-staff meeting to update the company on the crisis and give them general direction about behavior should they be contacted by the media or others.
- Finance makes purchased services easily available.
- The marketing department creates a media buy to state the case and support the brand in this time of crisis.

What Went Wrong and What Could Have Been Corrected in the AIDS Crisis?

1. PREPAREDNESS. It shouldn't take a genius to know that an organization could anticipate an AIDS-related crisis at the height of an AIDS epidemic. Just as it should not take a genius to prepare for COVID-related crises. They are certainly not likely BULL SHARK events. But, this organization didn't think even on the surface about a potential AIDS-related crisis. It may not have surfaced a pediatric emergency physician with AIDS, but it could have thought of other doctors, especially surgeons, to have AIDS (or nurses or aides or anyone coming in contact with patients and their families).

2. LEGAL. When a person has been accused of an illness such as AIDS, many laws of confidentiality apply. That would clearly necessitate the need for legal counsel. But, this was complicated because of patient contact, contact with children. It has high emotional issues, as you might expect. This was a case of, "Damned if you do, damned if you don't." In this case, and given the pleasing personality of the physician, we were advised to tell the doctor about the anonymous call and let him respond. He responded very positively and suggested having an AIDS test. Not everyone will cooperate so willingly. A lot of physicians, think surgeons, have high egos and might not have reacted so politely. We were able to dodge a bullet as it turns out because the doctor tested negative.

3. COMMUNICATIONS. In this case, communication was most critical. The important parties were brought together to deliberate at length about a course of action. What words must be used? Who would interact with the physician? Where would this take place? When would this take place? How would we follow up if he tested positive? How would we tell the various publics? Ultimately everyone would know, especially if the news media pressed the matter. The doctor's reputation, and potentially his practice, would have been ruined.

4. AFTER ACTION REPORT. Again, believe it or not, no formal crisis team was created and no crisis support team. No brainstorming took place and no plans developed. The organization essentially waited for the next crisis to happen.

Discussion Questions

1. Do you have a plan in place regarding an employee with a communicable disease?

2. Does your plan regard interactions between employees and the public?

3. Is your organization an open one? Will employees share information?

4. Would a "whistle blower" feel safe in your organization?

5. Is your organization vulnerable to this kind of crisis?

6. Do you have a crisis support team?

PART 2

From Prevention to Management to Recovery

CHAPTER 6

Crisis Defined

A crisis arrives anytime and usually out of nowhere. It accelerates at different speeds and in different delivery systems, as well as at different hours. It affects the company reputation, finances, and future. It can be internal in nature or external and present danger as well as an opportunity. Ultimately, it's a "turning point." The old Greek word for crisis means turning point. Think for a minute about 9/11. It created a turning point on earth. Nothing was the same afterward as it had been before, especially with travel and feelings of safety. The Tylenol crisis created a turning point in retail packaging.

Many books have been published about crisis management. Most of them are theoretical in nature and lack the experience of someone who has suffered through crisis, especially Bull Shark crises. Having experienced several Bull Shark events, I can tell you from firsthand experience that crises are deeply unsettling and fluid. They typically don't repeat themselves although themes do. I offer here an outline of how you feel when crisis strikes, how you can define a crisis so that you know you're really in one, what simple things you must accomplish, the people you need to be responsible to, what your messages to them will be, the kind of materials you will need at your disposal, and an understanding of the media and how it operates. Let's begin with how you will feel when you are in a crisis:

- **Time collapses:** You will feel the pressure of the clock. Time will fly as you hurry to meet deadlines and act to contain the fires that have arisen around you. You run on adrenaline and then you will feel fatigue as the pressures and stresses help to produce cortisol in your brain.

- **Decisions must be made quickly:** The many decisions you make must be made quickly and as smartly as possible. Everything will feel in flux. You will likely juggle many needs at the same time.

- **Specific threats are identified:** You will need to identify the most important threats and deal with them first in a triage fashion.

- **Urgent demands are made for information:** Everyone—everyone—will want your voice and your ear. You will succeed in the end if you communicate regularly. You need to be visible, patient, and emotionally intelligent.

- **A sense of a loss of control prevails:** You will be lucky if you feel in control of the entire situation. That said, you will use intuition and likely make mistakes. It's part of the deal; accept it.

- **Pressure builds constantly:** The pressure will not relent. It will come from every direction, the top, the bottom, and the sides.

- **Demands are made for someone to blame:** More than anything people will want to hold someone accountable. Accept the blame. Settle this quickly or it will fester.

- **Reputations suffer:** Manage your message so that you can do the least damage to your reputation and the reputation of your organization.

- **Money loss and/or loss of life occur:** Accept early on that you will spend money and lose money. If you try too hard to manage money, in the long run, you will lose more than you think.
- **Communications are harder to manage:** Sometimes you will feel like your audiences are not hearing your message. Add to that, you will have different audiences with different concerns and that you must address all of them. This will be your hardest task, managing the message.

Three Phases of a Crisis

1. INITIAL PUBLIC PHASE

   This happens at the beginning of a crisis and offers an opportunity for the leaders to use influence and persuasion in a charismatic way to motivate staff to respond positively to the crisis, to assure audiences of efforts underway to correct any problems, and to comfort any afflicted parties. It's an opportunity for leaders to demonstrate leadership to the media who will mold public opinion.

2. OPERATIONAL PHASE

   During this phase of the crisis, leadership will understand the problem, assess the damages, create operational responses, manage messages, budgets, and other resources to create stability. In this stage, the crisis support team will manage most details involving equipment, logistics, personnel, and purchasing, among other necessary items.

3. ASSESSMENT PHASE

   When the crisis has been brought under control, organizations must assess their activities and answer questions, such as: How might we have anticipated this? How did our communication system work? Where did it break down? How did the public perceive us? Did we have a baseline for that understanding? What extraordinary resources did we use? What was the cost of this experience?

CHAPTER 7

How to Prevent a Crisis

Despite the Bull Sharks that loom below the waters of every organization, many crises can be prevented. How does this happen? It requires an organization to be enlightened and progressive. It requires organizations to follow this approach:

Invite

Executives often isolate themselves from others, not because they don't like people or respect them but because they run out of time going from one meeting to another. As a result, they have little to no contact with people who are closest to the business being done, to the customers they are serving, and to the potential problems that often lead to crises. To deal with this, executives, and managers, to some extent, must close the gap between themselves and the employees at the farthest end of the company spectrum. If management is going to meet, as we know they spend most of their time doing, they need to meet with the employees and customers farthest away from them. They need to carve out some time and create a meeting environment where all staff feel comfortable talking about things that should change so that crises can be averted.

Meet

Management needs to invite a variety of people from the organization and set a simple agenda. It is best that one topic be discussed: "What do you see in your everyday work that, if not done properly, might lead to a crisis?" In the meeting, bosses should not be present as we all know that they might inhibit staff from speaking. Refreshments should be served and a room with comfortable chairs be chosen. It's critical that the staff feel as relaxed as possible and that the meeting be facilitated in such a way that free brainstorming is possible.

Ask the Right Questions

How Do We Reduce Risk?

As the *Harvard Business Review* (*HBR*) says, "Risk is more abundant than ever … a strong risk function is the name of the game for today's leading businesses. This starts with an objective risk assessment and a dispassionate and aggressive closure of gaps. Companies are working to diversify supply chains, to make sure that they aren't concentrated in certain parts of the world, to automate and outsource, to mitigate inflation, and to invest to close gaps. Proactive risk management is more of an asset than ever before, and companies that successfully manage risk will likely be undeterred in their pursuit of profitable growth. Successful risk management is entirely within a company's own control."

5 Questions for Business Leaders to Ask in Uncertain Times (hbr.org)

HBR ASKS THESE QUESTIONS OF FRONTLINE WORKERS

"How can I help you?"

"Why are we doing it this way?"

"How are we doing in living out our values?"

Other Questions

What are we doing that we shouldn't be doing?

What are we doing that might get us in trouble?

What processes or equipment are likely to compromise us?

Listen

Again, the *HBR*, in an article by Erika James and Lynn Perry Wooten, gives us good advice: "How leaders navigate a crisis—big or small—has an enormous influence over the impact that crisis will have on their organization, not to mention the personal impact it will have on the people and leadership of that organization, in its aftermath."

What do top executives have in common? "When crises land," the authors say, "...they seek out and act on the counsel of *other people*. And lots of them.

"Human beings are imperfectly equipped to make rational decisions, and even less so when something as unexpected and devastating ... We are each of us prone to certain ways of thinking—heuristics and biases that are hard-wired into our behavior—which make it hard for us as individuals to see all the edges of a crisis, to understand its mutability, to chart all the possibilities (the opportunities as well as the risks) and to decide on the best course of action. We tend to downplay or dismiss threats along the lines of "it'll never happen to me, and even if it does, it won't be that bad." And when the chips finally do fall, we can become anchored to one particular plan or solution, even as the crisis shifts or changes direction. We may continue down one path long after it makes sense to do so, because of sunk costs: "we've come this far; it's too late to change course.

"Then there's the echo chamber. Whether we know it or not, most of us gravitate to people (and information) that confirm things we already think and believe. We're drawn to individuals and ideas that concur with, and even end up shaping, our worldview. The pandemic era has revealed worrying fault lines in the United States and elsewhere.

Intensifying political schisms, social unrest, and general divisiveness point to massive-scale confirmation bias—a vast shoring up of beliefs along socio-economic and racial lines that have created a crisis of polarization.

"Breaking out of the echo chamber and correcting for preconceptions isn't intuitive nor is it easy. But it's essential in a crisis, because a crisis is hard to predict and understand in all of its dimensions. A crisis seldom plays by your established rulebook or existing structures. Unchecked, a crisis can evolve, expand, and engulf in ways we will struggle to imagine or anticipate. For this reason, when a crisis hits, you need your leadership to be as bias-free, elastic, deft, and dynamic as the circumstances rapidly unfolding around you and your organization."

"The more eyes you have on the situation, the less likely it is that you will remain entrenched in your own thinking or anchored to one solution or plan," says the *HBR*. "And the more people you can turn to for counsel as the crisis develops, the easier it will be to shift course and adapt as exigencies dictate ... So how do you ensure you leverage the perspective of others now, before the next crisis hits you and your organization? Here are three questions to ask yourself:

1. **Do you currently have access to diverse voices and sources of information within your team or organization, or even beyond its boundaries?**
2. **Do you routinely build other team members' ideas or feedback into your decision-making?**
   Be honest about this. How amenable are you to other people's input? And do you always seek the same counsel or are you open to hearing from a diversity of input?
3. **What systems or processes might you need to put into place to surface and capture multistakeholder perspectives?**

"Look at how communication is structured in your organization and whether there are silos that you need to address. Is the flow of knowledge multilateral? How might you ensure that you hear voices other than those of your immediate team. In the age of Zoom and Teams, the workplace has become meeting-intensive, so what other mechanisms might you use to capture good ideas from a diversity of perspectives?"

In a Crisis, Great Leaders Prioritize Listening (hbr.org)

Listening Is an Overlooked Skill

According to Melissa Daimler who writes in the *HBR,* "Listening is an overlooked tool that creates an environment of safety when done well. Several studies over the decades have estimated that we spend anywhere from a third to half our time listening. And yet we don't retain very much. Back in 1957, researchers found that listeners only remembered about half of what they'd heard immediately after someone finished talking. There's no reason to think that ratio has improved since then.

"Listening can be a challenging skill to master. In our management development sessions, we find it helpful to highlight three levels of listening:

Internal listening is focused on your own thoughts, worries, and priorities, even as you pretend you're focusing on the other person.

Focused listening is being able to focus on the other person, but you're still not connecting fully to them.

360 listening. You're not only listening to what the person is saying, but how they're saying it—and, even better, what they're *not* saying, like when they get energized about certain topics or when they pause and talk around others.

"So how can we listen more? Three suggestions to try this week:

Look people in the eye. Put down your phone when you're in meetings. Close your laptop. See if you're more energized about work and the people with whom you work.

Create space in your day. Manage your calendar and stop booking yourself out the entire day. Give yourself time for reflection and space throughout the day, so that when you are talking with someone, you can give them your full attention.

Ask more questions. Next time a colleague or employee asks for advice, make sure you're listening and understand the situation. Then, before answering, ask a question. Clarify what they really need—usually it's just validation that their thinking is on the right track."

Listening Is an Overlooked Leadership Tool (hbr.org)

Act

Armed with many ideas about potential problems and crises, management must cull them to find those that suggest impending trouble and act to prevent trouble from happening. This requires a dedicated leader/ team to surface all potential crises.

Study Past Crises

Use the TYLENOL CRISIS as your guide. It was truly a Bull Shark event. That crisis will tell you to BE OPEN, HONEST, and ACCESSIBLE. TYLENOL will tell you to DEFER to the public and its safety and concerns and to defer to your mission and philosophy. The Tylenol crisis will also encourage you to IGNORE the financial concerns. Johnson & Johnson lost millions of dollars and all market share. But, they gained it back because of their attitude and behavior.

Examine all other crises, or appoint someone to be your crisis expert and empower that person with your crisis planning. Learn from the mistakes and successes of others.

Let's examine some of those to see what we can learn to adopt and to avoid. Let's begin with Tylenol, probably the gold standard for crisis response.

The Tylenol Crisis

The date was September 28, 1982. After taking Extra-Strength Tylenol, a young Chicago girl died. The next day, six more people complained of sickness from taking Tylenol and eventually died. A public health nurse visited the home of victims and found a recently purchased Tylenol bottle. She suspected the capsules and turned them over to authorities who found that they contained cyanide. Public health authorities told the public not to use Tylenol.

Johnson & Johnson took control of the situation by sending warnings to hospitals and distributors and halting Tylenol production and advertising. Then, when other incidents took place, Johnson & Johnson recalled all Tylenol products everywhere, something like 31 million bottles, valued at $100 million. At the time of the scare, the company's market share fell from 35 percent to 8 percent. Johnson & Johnson also spent a ton on advertising nationally telling people not to use any of its products with acetaminophen.

Johnson & Johnson was applauded for its efforts, especially after it opened itself to and worked with Chicago Police, the FBI, and the FDA. Tylenol came back strong within 12 months by reintroducing capsules in a new, triple-sealed package. Eventually the product regained the highest market share for this type of pain reliever in America.

Danger and Opportunity

The Chinese characters for the word "Crisis" include both "danger" and "opportunity." Johnson & Johnson proved that to be true. They certainly encountered danger but out of that came an opportunity, one that changed the nature of retailing, tamper-resistant packaging. Not only did they deal with the crisis, they found a way to prevent it from happening again. Tampering with products also became a federal crime. And, retailers replaced capsules with the "caplet," a tablet made to look like a capsule.

This Is What We Believe

Johnson & Johnson leaders said they acted in accordance with their Credo, as restated here:

We believe that our first responsibility is to the patients, doctors and nurses, to mothers and fathers, and all others who use our products and services. In meeting their needs everything we do must be of high quality. We must constantly strive to provide value, reduce our costs, and maintain reasonable prices. Customers' orders must be serviced promptly and accurately. Our business partners must have an opportunity to make a fair profit.

We are responsible to our employees who work with us throughout the world. We must provide an inclusive work environment where each person must be considered as an individual. We must respect their diversity and dignity and recognize their merit. They must have a sense of security, fulfillment, and purpose in their jobs. Compensation must be fair and adequate and working conditions clean, orderly, and safe. We must support the health and well-being of our employees and help them fulfill their family and other personal responsibilities. Employees must feel free to make suggestions and complaints. There must be equal opportunity for employment, development, and advancement for those qualified. We must provide highly capable leaders and their actions must be just and ethical.

We are responsible to the communities in which we live and work, and to the world community as well. We must help people be healthier by supporting better access and care in more places around the world. We must be good citizens—support good works and charities, better health and education, and bear our fair share of taxes. We must maintain in good order the property we are privileged to use, protecting the environment and natural resources.

Our final responsibility is to our stockholders. Business must make a sound profit. We must experiment with new ideas. Research must be carried on, innovative programs developed, investments made for the future, and mistakes paid for. New equipment must be purchased, new facilities provided, and new products launched. Reserves must be created to provide for adverse times. When we operate according to these principles, the stockholders should realize a fair return. www.jnj.com/our-credo.

www.ou.edu/deptcomm/dodjcc/groups/02C2/Johnson%20&%20Johnson.htm.

What Can You Learn From Other's Tragedies?

Could Johnson & Johnson have anticipated that crisis? You decide. Did they ever invest the time to consider their vulnerabilities? It's questionable. They probably had a risk management department, but that group was likely more concerned about liability regarding the typical lawsuits that came from people ingesting too many capsules or about on-the-job accidents, and the like.

It Takes Imagination

It takes imagination for a company like Johnson & Johnson to imagine that some mentally unstable person might place cyanide in the capsules of their pain reliever. It takes a kind of perverse imagination, the ability to think of the strange. The primary argument of this book is that someone must do this, imagine things that can't be easily imagined, like a Bull Shark attack in the rivers of Pittsburgh, Pennsylvania. Many crises should be easy to imagine, like the oil spills.

Take the Exxon Valdez for Instance

Supertankers roam the high seas regularly and one would think, plan for a possible accident. Exxon owned a supertanker, the Exxon Valdez, that was destined for California in March 1989 when it struck a reef near Alaska and spilled millions of gallons of crude oil in a few days. In the days to come, it caused the death of much of the natural wildlife and habitat.

The causes of the oil spill were many, but mostly related to human error; the National Transportation Safety Board determined that the crew was incompetent and overworked. The company failed to supervise the ship's master and the crew. The captain was not navigating the ship and media reported that the captain was intoxicated at the time of the crash, although he was later cleared of that charge.

In any event, the spill was an ecological disaster and could have been avoided. No amount of crisis planning could have prevented it, but Exxon could have dealt with it better. For instance, Exxon was criticized when it failed to respond quickly enough to the problem and its CEO did not arrive on the scene to evaluate and respond to the crisis. As one of the largest corporations in the world, Exxon seemed to be more concerned with its shareholders and less concerned with the environment.

https://en.wikipedia.org/wiki/Exxon_Valdez_oil_spill

Then There Was the Deepwater Spill

BP owned the off-shore deepwater site on America's Gulf Coast that poured millions of gallons into the ocean. If that wasn't bad enough, BP's CEO, Tony Hayward, said some blatantly insensitive things. For instance, during what became the worst oil spill in history, he complained, saying, "There's no one who wants this over more than I do. I want my life back." This he said when his company had effectively destroyed the lives and work of many people in the Gulf Coast, not to mention killing 11 BP workers.

What Can You Learn—Prepare the CEO!

Hayward, the CEO, sounded like he was trying to minimize the oil spill and its effect. For instance, at one point he said, "The Gulf of Mexico is a very big ocean. The amount of volume of oil and dispersant we are putting into it is tiny in relation to the total water volume." He added to that this incredible statement, "I think the environmental impact of this disaster is likely to have been very, very modest," adding that "The oil is on the surface. There aren't any plumes." (Scientists gave much proof of the error of this statement). BP employees and other workers reported being very ill during the cleanup, but Hayward said, "I'm sure they were genuinely ill, but whether it was anything to do with dispersants and oil, whether it was food poisoning or some other reason for them being ill, who knows." Then, as often happens, private comments to BP executives were reported. He allegedly said, "What the hell did we do to deserve this?"

www.britannica.com/event/Deepwater-Horizon-oil-spill

en.wikipedia.org/wiki/Deepwater_Horizon_oil_spill

CHAPTER 8

Learn to "Race!"

Respond. Assess. Communicate. Evaluate

DO THESE THINGS

- Get to the scene immediately.
- Assess the damage.
- Communicate ceaselessly.
- Evaluate as you go along.

Respond

If you don't respond immediately, you look as if you don't care. It's the CEO who must respond, not an underling. The CEO is the face of the company. She or he needs to be fearless, not thinking about or worried about saving her or his job. If things have been done correctly, a plan exists complete with enough details to make the work easier.

Assess

The CEO needs to have specific and concrete details about the situation. It is wise never to speculate. The CEO needs to be thinking OUT-SIDE-IN. That is, the CEO must think about the damage and harm done to the audience, not the company, when speaking to the media. (The message changes a little when the CEO addresses the company employees, board, and others.)

Communicate

At the onset of a crisis, the CEO must communicate ceaselessly. The messages must be attuned to the audiences. The first message is always: What exactly happened? When did it happen? Where did it happen? Why did it happen? How is the crisis and its aftermath being handled? What resources are being brought to bear on the matter? What will be done to see that this doesn't happen again? Then:

- Apologize.
- Extend concern to affected parties.
- Ask for support.
- Give regular updates.
- Communicate with sensitivity. Explain to the CEO the result of responding offensively or inappropriately.

Know What Good Communication Means

A newly appointed CEO of a hospital instituted a literacy exam for the cleaning staff of the hospital, many of whom had worked there in excess of 10 years and for whom English was a second language. At the same time, a newspaper article revealed that the same CEO had one of the highest compensation packages of CEOs in the region, including those at larger hospitals. At a town hall meeting with employees, an employee questioned the fairness of laying off these cleaning staff while the CEO received an overly generous salary. The CEO responded that the employees should be happy that they worked in a hospital that had a woman as a CEO. Clearly, the CEO showed no sensitivity toward the cleaning staff workers, some of whom had worked in the hospital for many years. Many employees lost respect for the CEO which she never regained.

Evaluate

During the crisis, much information must be recorded. Certainly, Marketing and PR must record all interactions, in the news media as well as all social media. Companies can hire agencies to do this.

Run a Drill

You can call it a "DRY RUN" or "maneuvers"; call it anything, but do it. PRACTICE ... Practice ... Practice. Bull Sharks exist and they surface. Know where everyone goes, what they do when they get there, and what they say, if anything. Prepare for the Bull Sharks. Stretch your imagination.

The armed forces have their "War Games," a way of testing their responses to conflict situations. In the 1960s, the U.S. military practiced responses related to the Berlin Wall crisis. Members of NATO have considered war games regarding future conflicts with Russia and China. They probably also consider scenarios involving North Korea.

Some famous and bright people have spoken on the need for planning:

- "Plan for what is difficult while it is easy, do what is great while it is small."—Sun Tzu
- "The future belongs to those who prepare for it today."—Malcolm X
- "By failing to prepare, you're preparing to fail."—Benjamin Franklin
- "Give me six hours to chop down a tree and I will spend the first four sharpening the axe."—Abraham Lincoln
- "Another way to be prepared is to think negatively. Yes, I'm a great optimist. But, when trying to make a decision, I often think of the worst-case scenario ... one thing that makes it

possible to be an optimist, is if you have a contingency plan
for when all hell breaks loose. There are a lot of things I don't
worry about, because I have a plan in place if they do."—Randy
Pausch, Carnegie Mellon University (CMU)

• "An ounce of prevention is worth a pound of cure."—Benjamin
Franklin

The university where I teach has drills, as do many other organizations. At CMU, we receive messages from time to time like this one:

Dear Members of the Carnegie Mellon Community:

The university's Emergency Preparedness and Response Team will conduct an emergency response training exercise at Hunt Library tomorrow from 8 a.m. to noon. This practice exercise, which is designed to simulate an active police response, is intended to practice and test our emergency response protocols in coordination with external emergency agencies to help ensure the safety and well-being of our community should we ever face a real emergency.

This is only a drill. The CMU community will NOT be in any danger.

As part of the training exercise, emergency vehicles and response activities will be near Hunt Library. We will post signage nearby to remind members of our community that a drill is in progress. This practice exercise has been designed to minimize the impact to classes or events in the library or nearby buildings. However, Hunt Library will be closed from 8 a.m. to noon and Frew Street will be closed from 7:15 to 10 a.m. for the training exercise. If you have any questions about this emergency response training exercise, please contact us.

This practice exercise has been designed to minimize the impact to classes or events in the library or nearby buildings. However, Hunt Library will be closed from 8 a.m. to noon and Frew Street will be closed from 7:15 to 10 a.m. for the training exercise. If you have any questions about this emergency response training exercise, please contact us.

How Do You Run a Drill?

Create a Situation

The crazier the situation the better. Think outrageously. Think outside the normal routines of the organization. Be weird.

Limit Time and Contact

Put the pressure on. Involve people who are in different parts of the world, in different time zones. Make the team sweat. Use actors to simulate the media and the aggrieved. Make it as real as possible.

Respond

Write a media release. Write messages to employees and others. Have the spokesperson give a media conference.

Evaluate Response

Be critical of your performances. Create evaluations tools ahead of time. Be tough on the process, not on each other.

Determine What Worked and What Didn't

Be honest. Make some critiques anonymous if you want to. You'll not learn by being indirect.

Fix Those That Didn't Work

Fix processes now or suffer the consequences later. Look, ultimately you don't want a crisis to happen. If you can avoid one, you're truly better off. But, when they occur, and they do occur, you'll be much better off when you know how to respond.

Plan Another Drill

Malcolm Gladwell cited research that said to become an expert you need to practice 10,000 times. Well, not 10,000 in this case but as many as feasible.

What Else Did You Learn?

1. You can't hide from a crisis.
2. You must place others' concerns above your own.
3. You can never speculate.
4. You must partner with other entities (police, government agencies, media, etc.).
5. You can't worry about money.
6. You must overcommunicate.
7. You must never quibble.
8. You must plan for crisis.
9. You must find your Bull Sharks.
10. You must practice for the day when your Bull Shark surfaces.

Discussion Questions

1. Did the organizations discussed in this chapter see their vulnerabilities?

2. Do you have similar vulnerabilities?

3. How well did their spokesperson respond?

4. Did they engage or enrage the media?

5. Did the organizations respond quickly and appropriately enough?

6. Did the spokesperson answer the important questions: who, what, when, where, why, how, and how much?

7. Did the organization apologize and was it sincere?

CHAPTER 9

Management—How to Navigate Through Crises in Real Time

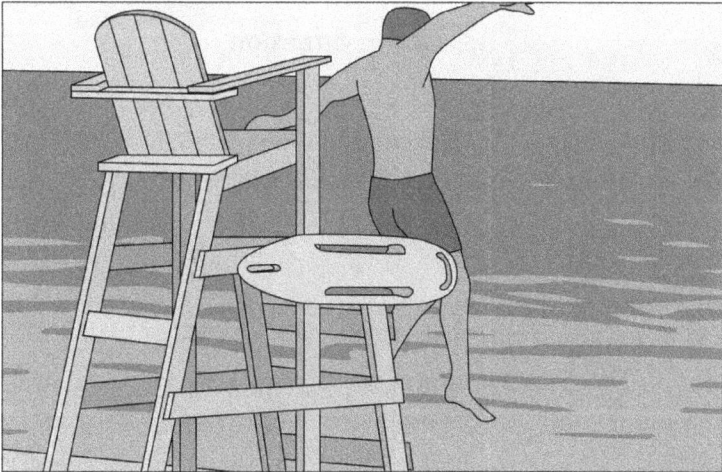

When you are in the midst of a crisis, time distorts. Everything seems to be happening at once. Demands come from all sides. Nerves are frayed. Every question seems like an interrogation. You wait to see what bad thing will happen next; what revelation of wrongdoing will surface. A three-hour meeting is the norm. Enemies come out of nowhere and friends seem to disappear. You fall into catastrophic thinking. Only the coolest heads prevail.

How do you get through the horror of crisis? If you have crisis plans in place, as you most certainly should, you can use the plans to guide you. Plans will tell you to assemble your crisis team and provide you with the many tools a good plan will include: the crisis support team, media contact lists, important phone numbers, useful talking points, and so on. But, first, someone needs to take control and assess the situation so as to have a timely response.

Respond

Say something. Don't hide in the office. People will want to hear from you, if only to say that you are getting all of the information and trying to discover what has happened as you take precautions that everything is under control. Say that your first concern is for the people affected and for your employees and the general public.

Assess the Situation

The first obligation of the crisis team will be to assess the situation. The team must gather as much information as possible. Is there physical damage? Was anyone injured? Will there likely be any emotional damage? If the answer to any of these questions is yes, the obvious course of action requires immediate attention from skilled professionals—engineers, physicians, counselors, allied health care professionals, and other experts. If there are no life-threatening issues, is there brand damage? If so, how extensive is it? What is the mass media saying? What's happening on social media? What is happening to our sales in real time? What important operational data can be accessed quickly? What are our vendors thinking? Our neighbors? Professional organizations to which we belong?

Contain the Situation

If there are physical damages (think oil spills, computer hacking, and poisonings), find ways to minimize the damages so that they don't expand or reoccur. Again, the best way to manage a crisis is to prepare for it—to plan. With a plan in place that directs people to perform critical actions, a crisis can seem more like a controlled event. Government agencies, such as the Federal Emergency Management Agency (FEMA) in the United States, exist for this reason, to respond to the kinds of emergencies that are likely to occur. When FEMA works well, it typically has planned for the emergencies that it responds to—floods, hurricanes, wild fires, and so on. But, even FEMA experiences Bull Shark events. In any event, someone has to try to put the brakes on the problem. This requires decisive action, decision making, and a ton of effective communication.

Communicate—Communicate—Communicate

From the top, it is critical that the leadership (the CEO and crisis team) ask questions and listen. As a result, executives will be better prepared to take the right action and offer accurate information to all audiences. These audiences will differ as organizations and their constituents differ. A good crisis plan will have already outlined the audiences and their concerns. (This book offers a separate section on communication—target audiences, messages, media, feedback review, cultural considerations, and noise.)

Executives must check and double check the information they receive. The best way to think about the information needs is to think of the 5Ws—who, what, when, where, and why (with how and how much added). Who is involved (all audiences). What happened? When did this occur? Where did it occur? Why did this happen? (Here it is important to speak ONLY to what is factual with no assumptions or speculation being made.) How are you dealing with it? How much will this cost? The basic questions must be answered along with questions associated with them.

Again, a good crisis plan will list all audiences, the messages they want/need to hear, the medium by which they must hear the messages, the timing of those messages, the messengers who will deliver the messages, and the venues where the messages will be delivered.

Executives must have patience by the boatload. They cannot argue with anyone, especially the media. They can firmly assert the facts, but they must never become defensive. In a crisis, an organization needs the media as a partner, a partner who can help an organization reach vital audiences with vital information. And, it's worth noting that correct information needs to filter through the organization in the event that media contact staff and, of course, so that staff is informed and able to help where possible.

Be Present

In a crisis, the executives must be ALL IN. They must be on the scene, literally and figuratively, 24/7. Harry Truman, an American president, had a sign on his desk that said, "The buck stops here." He realized that no matter who caused a crisis, he had to take responsibility for it. Typically, the CEO becomes the spokesperson. The CEO must either have experience addressing the media or have been trained rigorously to do so. Most people are dissatisfied with anyone other than the CEO speaking for the organization in a crisis. And, many CEOs feel uncomfortable with the role; that's why prior training is critical. If an organization is OPEN, HONEST, and ACCESSIBLE, it will generally receive the support and assistance of the media and everyone else with a voice. Trying to hide, obfuscate, obscure, or delay will create doubters and negativity. TIMELINESS and ACCURACY are critical.

Visit the Site

For those crises that are off site, the CEO must appear at the scene to assess the damage and offer appropriate apologies, if necessary. Too often, as in the case of the East Palestine, Ohio Rail Disaster in 2023, President Joe Biden waited too long to appear and show concern. As *The Guardian* wrote, "Joe Biden on Friday surveyed the federal cleanup in East Palestine, Ohio, *more than a year after an explosive fire from a derailed train carrying hazardous chemicals—and the president saw up close the lingering hostility from victims still angry that he had waited so long to visit.* (Italics added.) The White House has said Biden was waiting for the right moment to visit."

www.theguardian.com/us-news/2024/feb/17/biden-east-palestine-ohio-2023-rail-disaster

Care About What You See

It should go without saying that a CEO needs empathy. Some writers have suggested that empathy is the #1 trait a successful CEO must have. Empathy means understanding, not just your own emotions, but, more importantly, in a crisis, understanding the emotions of others. How could you not feel for people whose environment has been poisoned?

As Boston.com said in an article about CEOs saying dumb things, "Tony Hayward was CEO of British Petroleum during the Deepwater Horizon oil spill that affected the Gulf of Mexico. An explosion killed 11 oil workers on the rig and oil began to leak from the ocean floor. Hayward and BP initially downplayed the effects of the spill, saying the environmental impact would be "very, very modest" on May 17, 2010. On May 30, 2010, Hayward told a reporter, "There's no one who wants this thing over more than I do, I'd like my life back." He was widely criticized for the remarks that were seen as insensitive to those immediately impacted by the spill. Hayward was replaced as BP's CEO later that year.

www.boston.com/news/jobs/2014/04/08/when-ceos-do-say-dumb-things/

CHAPTER 10

Expect Anything to Happen and Plan for It

Plans are worthless, but planning is everything.
—Dwight D. Eisenhower, former U.S. President and
Commander-in-Chief during WWII

In a 2018 Deloitte survey of organizations from around the globe, 47 percent of those without a crisis management plan reported that their finances were negatively impacted by a recent crisis, compared to 31 percent of those that did have a plan.

www2.deloitte.com/uk/en/pages/risk/articles/2018-global-crisis-management-survey.html.

Similarly, a 2019 PwC global crisis survey of various organizations from different industries across the globe found that organizations that emerged stronger from a crisis had implemented preparatory measures (such as having a CMP in place) in anticipation of a crisis.

www.pwc.com/ee/et/publications/pub/pwc-global-crisis-survey-2019.pdf.

The bumper sticker says, "SH*T HAPPENS!" It does ... when you LEAST EXPECT IT ... at the MOST INCONVENIENT times. But, if you manage crises BEFORE THEY HAPPEN, you will manage them a lot better WHEN they happen!

What we're talking about here are Bull Shark events, those that aren't just unexpected and rare but totally unexpected, events you would never dream of happening, crazy, weird, totally uncalled-for events, crises that leave you dumbfounded.

You lost a woman's fetus? You gotta be kidding me. Who would have ever thought? You have a surgeon who's been operating on people and now has tested positive for AIDS? You gotta be kidding me. Who would have ever thought. The parking garage employees have been stealing money for years in a criminal enterprise? You gotta be kidding me. Who would have thought?

Who Would Have Thought?

The purpose of this book is to encourage organizations to brainstorm their vulnerabilities, not just the typical and common ones, but the outliers, the ones that lurk way in the background waiting to spring on you and cause you untold havoc. These are the Bull Sharks, swimming upstream, deep in the freshwaters waiting to take a nice chunk out of your midsection and drag you to the depths to finish the job.

What Are Your Bull Sharks? How Do You Surface Them?

Try this approach:

1. Believe that you can have Bull Shark events.
2. Appoint someone to lead an effort to identify Bull Sharks.

3. Integrate with risk management or other crisis planning activities.
4. Schedule a Bull Shark fishing session.
5. Brainstorm, ideate, imagine.

These Organizations Can Expect Crises

AIRLINES—We could fill a book about airline disasters. So many things can go wrong, despite the fact that airline travel is one of the safest ways to travel. Yet, when an airplane crashes or frightens customers with mechanical failures, the media rushes in to report the problems or cover the plane crash because of the vividness and terror of the situation.

FOOD PRODUCERS—Any time a food processor releases *E. coli* or some other deadly bacteria into its food, people panic. This happened with the world's largest beef producer. The same holds true for moments such as "Mad Cow" disease and "Hoof and Mouth" disease.

FINANCIAL FIRMS—Sometimes these companies make promises they can't keep and many of their customers lose money, especially their savings. This happens, of course, not just with firms but with individuals such as Bernie Madoff and Ponzi schemes.

CHEMICAL COMPANIES—Does the name Bhopal ring any bells? Union Carbide bought a terrible disaster to the Indian city of Bhopal with a major chemical disaster. Exxon Valdez and Deepwater have also taken their places in the annals of chemical disasters.

TECHNOLOGY BREAKDOWNS—Not a day go by that someone is reporting "hacking." Your organization can be hacked, in fact, it probably will be hacked. What will you do when your systems serve up the social security numbers of all your customers to some malicious terrorist?

Sh*t Will Happen to Small Companies as Well as Big Ones

Crises are not limited to Bull Shark events in size and severity. Most people suffer through what they feel is a crisis. They lose their passport while on vacation, perhaps, and they must deal with the fallout. A loved one dies unexpectedly, and the family is left with arrangements and discoveries. A tire goes flat in the middle of the night on a dark country road with no service station nearby. Things happen to all of us, corporations most publicly. CEOs say really dumb things. Lights go out in underground swimming pools, roadways flood, submersibles implode. Sh*t happens continuously.

Case in Point

Once upon a time there was a very, very popular restaurant in Pittsburgh, family-owned and serving delicious food. If you know Pittsburgh, you know that it's a city of small, well-defined neighborhoods. There's Bloomfield, Squirrel Hill (yep, named after squirrels), North Side, South Side, Shadyside, East Liberty, Regent Square, and a few others.

This wonderful restaurant sat in one of these neighborhoods and despite not-so-great parking, had a thriving business. You definitely had to call for a reservation. Things went along smoothly for years and years until a Bull Shark event happened. You've probably already guessed if you read the introduction about the restaurant with the flying rats.

The restaurant was thriving until someone decided to build next to it. In order to build they had to raze some properties next to it. This was later surmised to have set the rats loose.

One evening as a couple was dining at the restaurant, a rat, walking across a ceiling beam, fell onto their table. You can imagine the reaction to the people who were disrupted. They screamed, threw up their napkins, and burst away from the table. The frightened rat also scurried away, his route taking him across the floor and observed by the other patrons.

This happened before the age of the internet, before Yelp, before Instagram, Facebook, and the rest. But, it didn't stop the word from traveling across Pittsburgh, Allegheny County, and adjoining cities and counties.

Who would have thought? A rat falling from a ceiling beam? Now that's a true Bull Shark event.

How does a small business predict such an event so as to be prepared to respond to it? It takes some serious deep thinking and imagination. Perhaps it could have been prevented then. Maybe the restaurant owners, when experiencing the contiguous construction and anticipating a rodent problem, could have gone to the builders and asked them to set traps. I worked in a building once that was contiguous to a building site that unleashed hundreds of cockroaches. I'm guessing that others have experienced such a thing. So, it would have been possible to imagine the rat scenario.

The restaurant, as may be guessed, never recovered from the incident and shut its doors not long after. No amount of advertising or PR could erase the image of a rat falling in someone's lap, or soup. It was too visual.

What Went Wrong and What Could Have Been Corrected in the Crisis?

1. PREPAREDNESS. With contiguous construction going on, the restaurant owners might have considered many strange things happening. However, having known several restaurant owners, I know what their days look like. They're up at 7 a.m. to meet vendors and prepare for the lunch business. They then have a window between lunch and dinner to clean up and prepare for the evening crowd. That doesn't leave them much time to think about what might go wrong. And then, they'll likely think about the obvious: food poisoning, irate customers, and staff with communicable diseases. But, like any organization, they must think more broadly.

2. COMMUNICATIONS. Communication was most critical to this restaurant. There was no way that the incident wouldn't go viral. It's likely that other customers saw what happened. Even if

they didn't, wouldn't you want to tell everyone you know what
had happened at your table? The restaurant needed immediate
communication with a variety of audiences. It needed to assume
a posture, perhaps one of humility and apology or perhaps one
of humor, after all, it did have an element of the ridiculous
about it. In any event, depending on the approach it took, the
restaurant needed to immediately schedule advertising so as to
reach the broadest audience most quickly. It needed characters
such as the director of the department of health, the restaurant
inspector, perhaps even the people who witnessed the event.

3. LEGAL. This organization could only focus on the legal
    ramifications of their Bull Shark event. Let's face it; rats and
    vermin of any sort don't mix well with food and restaurants,
    although most restaurants struggle with the problem and we
    probably don't want to know what's really in our food. Movies
    like "Casino" show scenes of restaurant workers spitting in the
    sandwiches of police officers before serving them as take out.

    a. AFTER ACTION REPORT. This privately-owned
        restaurant, with perhaps 10 to 12 full-time employees did
        not have crisis plans, a crisis team, and they certainly had
        no crisis support team. No brainstorming took place, and
        no plans were ever developed. The organization essentially
        waited for the next crisis to happen. If they had done some
        crisis thinking, and knowing that construction was right
        next door, construction that would unearth some undesira-
        ble critters, they could have easily surfaced the rats.

No Fat People Allowed

According to Boston.com, "Michale Jeffries, the CEO of clothing
company Abercrombie & Fitch, landed in hot water … over comments
he made during a 2006 interview with Salon came to light. In the
interview, Jeffries opened up about his focus on 'attractive' people and
said he was OK with excluding heavier customers." In every school
there are the cool and popular kids, and then there are the not-so-cool
kids … Candidly, we go after the cool kids. We go after the attractive

all-American kid with a great attitude and a lot of friends." He went on to say, "A lot of people don't belong (in our clothes), and they can't belong. Are we exclusionary? Absolutely."

Those comments lit a firestorm for Jeffries and Abercrombie and Fitch, a popular retailer with young people.

The CEO of Lululemon, Dennis (Chip) Wilson, also put his mouth in his foot. As Boston.com reported, "The founder of yoga apparel company Lululemon Athletica found himself in the downward-facing doghouse last year when he responded to complaints that the pants were piling by saying, 'quite frankly some women's bodies just actually don't work for it' during an interview with Bloomberg TV last year. Wilson gets an honorable mention for his 2004 remarks in which he said he chose the name Lululemon for his company because he believed that Japanese people have a hard time pronouncing it. 'It's funny to watch them try and say it,' Wilson told the National Post Business Magazine."

www.boston.com/news/jobs/2014/04/08/when-ceos-do-say-dumb-things/.

Antisemitism at the Local Level

In the Mexican War Streets neighborhood of Pittsburgh's North Side in 2024, a man was caught on a doorbell camera writing antisemitic messages on the property of Jewish residents. This happened on the heels of the Israel–Hamas confrontations when university students and others were protesting Israel's response to earlier Hamas attacks. Elected officials in Pittsburgh had to respond quickly to the issue, especially in light of the growing problems on college campuses and in the context of a terrorist attack in Pittsburgh some six years earlier in October 2018.

In 2018, a shooting took place at the Tree of Life synagogue in the Squirrel Hill neighborhood of Pittsburgh and became news around the world. The congregation was attacked during Shabbat morning services; 46-year-old Robert Gregory Bowers killed 11 people and wounded 6, including several Holocaust survivors, creating the deadliest attack on any Jewish community in America.

The killer was shot multiple times by police and arrested at the scene. He was charged with 63 federal crimes to which he pleaded not guilty. On June 16, 2023, a jury found him guilty on all federal counts, and on August 3, 2023, he was sentenced to death by lethal injection. https://en.wikipedia.org/wiki/Pittsburgh_synagogue_shooting.

Given that context, the Mexican War Streets (named, ironically, after battles of the Mexican–American War) needed to act on the antisemitism on their streets. It was a crisis built on an international, national, and local crisis. It was a small but critical crisis for the small neighborhood and the city.

"Turn Around, Don't Drown"

Many crises occur all over the world that are water-related. In another water-related episode, in August 2011, rains caused flash floods on a major thoroughfare in Pittsburgh, Pennsylvania, trapping two women and two children in their cars where they drowned.

The drainage system on Washington Boulevard, a main road cutting across the city, couldn't handle the downpour and the water level rose to 9 feet in a matter of minutes.

Rescuers rowed in inflatable boats to reach drivers, though some swam to safety on their own as 2.1 inches of rain fell in an hour during the evening rush.

People were clinging to trees, poles, and car roofs, Pittsburgh's KDKA-TV reported. One woman tried to scramble to the roof of her car, but the water was moving so fast, she was dragged along in it where she was fortunately able to grab on to a truck.

FEMA distilled its advice in such situations to a slogan: "Turn around, don't drown."
https://nypost.com/2011/08/20/two-women-kids-killed-in-pittsburgh-flash-floods/.

FCK!

Imagine that you own one of the world's largest franchises, and you sell chicken. Now, imagine you run out of chicken in England and Ireland.

Yikes, what an unimaginable crisis that is! This happened to Kentucky Fried Chicken (KFC), a worldwide franchise of incredible success. But, for supply chain or other reasons, they ran out of chicken in one of their prime markets.

How did they respond to the crisis? According to *HuffPost*, "KFC took out full-page advertisements in United Kingdom newspapers ... to apologize for the fast-food chain's chicken shortage.

"The tongue-in-cheek ads featuring an empty chicken bucket emblazoned with **FCK** immediately won fans for clever humor ... The fowl shortage, which KFC attributed to delivery issues, forced the chain to close more than half of its 900 British restaurants this week. Angry customers called the police, and even—gasp—went to Burger King.

'A website link at the bottom of the ad list(ed) restaurants that have been supplied chicken, with the banner: 'The chicken crossed the road, just not to our restaurants ...'

"A KFC UK spokesperson told *HuffPost* the 'tongue-in-cheek rearrangement,' of the brand's letters was the company's 'first thought when we realized the impact of our closed restaurants on customers in the United Kingdom.'

www.huffpost.com/entry/kfc-says-fck-in-full-page-ad-apologizing-for-chicken-shortage_n_5a9034b1e4b0ee6416a2adfb.

The Bomb in the Car on the Campus—A Crisis Averted

The sirens screamed as five police cars followed the Datsun sedan into the campus parking lot. Campus police converged on the vehicle as it pulled to a stop, the horrified driver cowering in the driver's seat. A bomb squad vehicle appeared as an alert had gone out that the car contained a bomb. And, in fact, it did. It filled the entire backseat of the Datsun. All faculty, staff, and students were warned to stay inside. The bomb was easy to see. It was fragile and it appeared to be metallic and heavy. It looked just like a bomb with fins and a pointed snout, the kind that were dropped out of an airplane in World War II. The driver was petrified as police approached his car with guns drawn. They bent him over the front bumper of his car while he tried to explain that he was delivering the "bomb" to the university arts department where it was going to be used as a prop in a forthcoming play. Using caution, members of the bomb squad, attired in bomb defusing clothing approached the bomb and certified that it was made of cardboard.

Ocean Gate

According to Wikipedia, "On June 18, 2023, *Titan*, a submersible operated by the American tourism and expeditions company Ocean-Gate, imploded during an expedition to view the wreck of the *Titanic* in the North Atlantic Ocean off the coast of Newfoundland, Canada. Aboard the submersible were: Stockton Rush, the American chief executive officer of OceanGate; Paul-Henri Nargeolet, a French deep-sea explorer and *Titanic* expert; Hamish Harding, a British businessman; Shahzada Dawood, a Pakistani–British businessman; and Dawood's son Suleman.

"Communication between *Titan* and its mother ship, MV *Polar Prince*, was lost 1 hour and 45 minutes into the dive. Authorities were alerted when it failed to resurface at the scheduled time later that day. After the submersible had been missing for four days, a remotely operated underwater vehicle (ROV) discovered a debris field containing parts of *Titan*, about 500 m (1,600 ft) from the bow of the *Titanic*. The search area was informed by the United States Navy's (USN) sonar detection of an acoustic signature consistent with an implosion around the time communications with the submersible ceased, suggesting that the pressure hull had imploded while *Titan* was descending, resulting in the instantaneous deaths of all five occupants.

"The search and rescue operation was conducted by an international team led by the United States Coast Guard (USCG), USN, and Canadian Coast Guard.[1] Support was provided by aircraft from the Royal Canadian Air Force and United States Air National Guard, a Royal Canadian Navy ship, as well as several commercial and research vessels and ROVs.[2][3]

"Numerous industry experts had raised concerns about the safety of the vessel. OceanGate executives, including Rush, had not sought certification for *Titan*, arguing that 'excessive safety protocols and regulations hindered innovation.'

In a lengthy article following the disaster, the *New Yorker* magazine had this to say: "The primary task of a submersible is to not implode. The second is to reach the surface, even if the pilot is unconscious, with oxygen to spare. The third is for the occupants to be able to open the hatch once they surface. The fourth is for the submersible to be easy to find, through redundant tracking and communications systems, in case rescue is required. Only the fifth task is what is ordinarily thought of as the primary one: to transport people into the dark, hostile deep."

www.newyorker.com/news/a-reporter-at-large/the-titan-submersible-was-an-accident-waiting-to-happen.

And, finally, the Pittsburgh bagel shop that was reported to have mice droppings on their bagel, mice stuck in glue traps, and mice nests behind their ovens. How will they ever recover from that? It will take some major creativity and action!

CHAPTER 11

Use This Guide to Surface *Your* Bull Sharks and Plan for Them

This part is not easy. It requires open-mindedness and creativity as well as organization and management. Again, Bull Shark events are not just unexpected; they are nearly ridiculous to think about. "How could this ever happen?" The answer is: a lost fetus.

Organizations must commit the time and resources to identify their vulnerabilities, to dig deep, to imagine, and to bring many people into the process. If you delegate this task to an executive team only, you will miss the voices of the people closest to potential problems. Bring the secretaries, the environmental services, the lowest level of staff into the creative sessions and listen to them. Use their comments to imagine Bull Shark events.

Hire a facilitator and involve vendors. Consider bringing in customers. You'll never have the points of view you need to discover the really crazy potential problems if you delegate the discovery and planning to just the executive and managers. So, follow this approach:

A GUIDE FOR SURFACING BULL SHARK EVENTS

1. Appoint a facilitator.
2. Define Bull Shark event and give examples.
3. Introduce all attendees.
4. Define the agenda for the session:
   a. Open brainstorming;
   b. No topic taboo;
   c. No questioning/naysaying;
   d. Recording of all suggestions;
   e. Voting on six most likely Bull Shark events;
   f. Deep discussion of the six.
5. Begin brainstorming with a potential Bull Shark event and record as you go.
6. Choose the six most unexpected but possible Bull Shark events.
7. Discuss the six deeply, one at a time.
8. Discuss the planning process:
   a. What might happen?
   b. When might it happen?
   c. Where might it happen?
   d. Why is this likely to happen?
   e. How will the event be managed?
   f. Who are the crisis team, crisis support team?
   g. What logistics are necessary if the Bull Shark attacks?
   h. What resources will be required to manage the attack, financial and otherwise?
   i. Who will record the organization's Bull Shark responses?
   j. Who will own the plan?

Other Important Considerations for Surfacing Bull Sharks

With every day-to-day activity that executives must accomplish, they can be excused for putting crisis planning low on their to-do lists. But, when the crisis hits, they will have wished that they had anticipated it and at least had some plan in place to deal with it.

As executives who have had little contact with the media, on the one hand, and the lowest level employees on the other, they now come face-to-face with both. However, they can rectify this by considering the following:

1. The MOST IMPORTANT consideration is to invite those staff to attend the session who would ordinarily be the least likely to be considered people—the lower-level staff. Environmental services workers, those in the night shift as well as the day shift, must be invited, as well as security staff, secretaries, and others who see things daily that the executives miss.
2. The intrinsic value of serving on this team must be considered and can be satisfied by publicizing the brainstorming event and its members and then establishing a web link for others to submit ideas in exchange for both intrinsic and extrinsic rewards.
3. Set up extrinsic rewards for the six best Bull Shark ideas (free parking, employee of the month, paid day off, etc.).
4. Identify people who surface potential crises as "Bull Sharks."
5. Have a Bull Shark dinner or party each year for those who identify crisis possibilities.

Some Crazy Thinking

It takes crazy thinking to surface your potential Bull Sharks. You have to go on a trip of the imagination where you might encounter many oddities and weird thoughts. You have to allow those thoughts. You may surface a legitimate Bull Shark or a hat full of ridiculous ideas. You have to let them all flow. I did this while I was sitting in church. The notion came to me and I let it come. I didn't interrupt it.

The Center for Disease Control (CDC) lists possible crises (they call them "hazards" and "incidents"). These include (hazards) bioterrorism, chemical emergencies, infectious disease outbreaks, natural disasters and severe weather, radiation emergencies, and explosions, (incidents) biological incident, cyber incidents, food and agricultural incident, natural disaster, nuclear and radiological incident, oil and hazardous materials incident, and terrorism incident.

https://emergency.cdc.gov/hazards-specific.asp

I had the crazy idea that these viruses, bacteria, and germs (anthrax, botulism, brucellosis, plague, smallpox, tularemia) could be spread very easily in an unusual way, a way that I'm guessing hasn't occurred to anyone. Let me tell you how.

The Catholic Mass offers those who are eligible the "Body and Blood of Christ." They do this at the altar with the priest and/or eucharistic ministers handing the faithful the "Host," the bread, the wafer, the "Body of Christ." They do this not just at a Catholic Mass but also at other Christian denominations. Then, the ministers offer the "Blood of Christ," the wine that has been sanctified. Parishioners come to the altar and sip from the chalice.

In a moment of perversity, it occurred to me that a "parishioner," that is terrorist, could take the chalice and instead of drinking the wine release a mouthful of infection into the chalice. If he or she went first, they could infect those who came after, as well as the priest who generally drinks the remaining wine. If this were done at a mass of several hundred people, those who took the cup would be infected and would go home to infect others—family, friends, co-workers, or anyone they met. Perverse, isn't it. Obviously, the terrorist would succumb, but many of them are on suicide missions anyway. What do they care?

This is an example of a Bull Shark, something few, if anyone, would expect, arising out of the mind of a sick person (I feel sick having thought of it). Add to this my understanding of church leaders (of all religions); they don't do crisis thinking/planning. They probably don't go beyond thinking, "How do we respond if one of our clergy is accused of child molestation?" I trust they have crisis plans for that as it has happened too frequently in all religions and some other organizations.

If enough suicide people were found and they had access to enough poison (anthrax, botulism, smallpox), they could initiate a large-scale Bull Shark event. It's terrible to think about, right. But, it and many other crazy ideas need to be thought about and planned for.

Think about your organization for a minute. Let your mind run wild. What crazy thing could happen? Maybe you're at an airport and someone rents a car, drives it through a gate, onto the runaway, and rams into a plane just as it is landing. That can be imagined and planned for. Anything is possible at any scale.

Bull Shark events happen to individuals, too. A young man, a husband and father of toddlers, dies suddenly at the theater. Taken to the hospital, the doctors say he had an aneurysm. A wife and mother of three children who has believed that her marriage was flawless, learns that her husband who traveled for his work led a double life having a family in another city.

Why Can't We Anticipate Crises?

Could anyone have imagined that terrorists would hijack airplanes and in a suicidal rage commandeer them, kill pilots and passengers, and fly the planes into buildings? They may have, if they had stretched their imaginations. Actually, it was reported that at least one person in a position to do something about a possible 9/11 scenario thought about it, but was ignored as part of bureaucracy and interdepartmental competition.

Most people knew that airliners had been hijacked in the past. The earliest recorded plane hijacking occurred in 1910. A Hungarian aristocrat and geologist Baron Franz Nopcsa von Felső-Szilvás became the first person in history to hijack an airplane attempting to avoid persecution by communists. The former spy convinced the military to give him transit in an airplane and pulled a pistol on the pilot demanding to be flown to Vienna.

https://en.wikipedia.org/wiki/List_of_aircraft_hijackings.

Since that time there have been hundreds of hijackings, many of them ending tragically. Recall the Munich Olympic Games and its aftermath. As stated earlier, a Hollywood movie from 1996, "Executive Decision," dramatized terrorists hijacking a commercial flight with the intention of crashing it into Washington, District of Columbia, Dulles Airport, and spreading biochemicals over the east coast of America. So why did no one learn from all of this in order to prevent the tragedy of 9/11?

Lack of imagination. The same imagination we should be using right now to prevent Bull Sharks from arising out of the deep to destroy and disrupt.

Piracy on the High Seas

If you're a Tom Hanks fan, you probably watched "Captain Phillips." If you watched that movie, you saw piracy on the high seas. You saw the story of Richard Phillips who commanded the MV Maersk Alabama, a container vessel from Oman. Captain Phillip sees that his ship is being followed by Somali pirates and he radios for help. The next day, the pirates return and secure their ladder to the ship. Captain Phillips tells the crew to hide in the engine room as the pirates take the bridge and hold Phillips and the other crew members at gunpoint. Phillips is taken prisoner and the lifeboat he is in sails to Somalia. Finally a U.S. navy destroyer USS Bainbridge approaches. Phillips escapes and all ends well for him.

https://en.wikipedia.org/wiki/Maersk_Alabama_hijacking.

So, once again you'd think we'd learn something from the movies (and from previous piracy attempts). But, noooooo. As of this writing, shipping across the world is changing because of piracy on the high seas. Yemen's Houthi rebels have been attacking shipping in the Red Sea, and Moller-Maersk is in their cross hairs. The Red Sea accounts for as much as 15 percent, and Maersk has stopped using the route for shipping and the global supply chain is a mess.

Can a crisis like this be averted? You tell me. If it happened before, can't it happen again? If it happened before, shouldn't someone have created a plan to avoid it, or certainly to deal with it? Come on! It was a popular movie 10 years ago. I could have predicted it would happen a decade later. You could have. Tom Hanks could have. And, certainly the real Captain Phillips could have.

This isn't what I call a Bull Shark event. This is an accident waiting to happen. A Bull Shark event might have been that two angry whales teamed up to ram the Maersk vessel, one from each side. This is the kind of thinking required for Bull Shark events. Even a crew mutiny would seem within the realm of possibility and would need to be planned for. Or, a crew-wide case of botulism. These kinds of crises can easily be surfaced. Two crazy whales, on the other hand, lurk deep in the psyche, just like a Bull Shark lies deep in a freshwater river where no one expects to be attacked by one.

Munich

Attack on the Olympic Village

A day of terror began at 4:30 a.m. on September 5, 1972, when Palestinian militants scaled a fence surrounding the Olympic Village in Munich. Disguised as athletes and using stolen keys, they forced their way into the quarters of the Israeli Olympic team. As they attempted to enter, they forced a wrestling coach to lead them to the rooms of the remaining Israeli coaches and athletes. The militants had detailed plans of the Olympic Village and the location of the Israeli athletes.

The terrorists collected more hostages and at least two were killed. The terrorists demanded that authorities release Palestinians held in Israeli prisons, as well as other terrorists and fly them to the Middle East. Meanwhile, this had all been broadcast to people around the world. Finally, hostages were transported to an air base where police waited to ambush them.

Meanwhile, on the air base tarmac a Boeing 727 sat with police officers disguised as flight crew.

The officers were going to subdue the terrorists when they got on the plane, but the police unanimously chose to abandon their posts. They had planned for armored cars to help but they were, believe it or not, stuck in traffic. They had no good plan and the result was awful, a complete snafu.

Helicopters arrived late; the terrorists boarded the jet and found it empty. Knowing they had been duped they yelled to their fellow terrorists and bullets started flying. People were killed; the scene resembled the worst action movie. Incorrect information was coming from many quarters as people continued to die, most of them Israelis.

The German government and the Munich police ruled that the attack had been unavoidable. They exonerated themselves, even in the face of a report that had predicted the Black September attack. Prior to the Olympic Games, the Munich Olympics organizing committee had asked police psychologist Georg Sieber to create worst-case security scenarios.

As Wikipedia reports, "Among the 26 possibilities proposed by Sieber were attacks on the games by the Irish Republican Army, the Red Army Faction, ETA, and other terrorist groups. Sieber's *Situation 21* proposed that a dozen Palestinian gunmen would scale the fence of the Olympic Village at 5:00 a.m., seize Israeli hostages, kill one or two, and issue a demand for the release of prisoners from Israeli jails and an aircraft to fly them to the Middle East. The organizing committee determined that preparing for threats such as those proposed by Sieber would create a security environment that was not in keeping with their vision for the Games. Within hours of the attack on the Olympic Village, Sieber was dismissed from his advisory position by an administrative apparatus that had already begun working to conceal evidence of its mistakes."

Then, less than two months after the Munich disaster, Black September terrorists hijacked a Lufthansa Boeing 727 on its way from Damascus to Frankfurt and threatened to blow it up, with the crew and passengers, if their demands were not met.

https://en.wikipedia.org/wiki/Munich_massacre.

CHAPTER 12

Communication Is Crucial

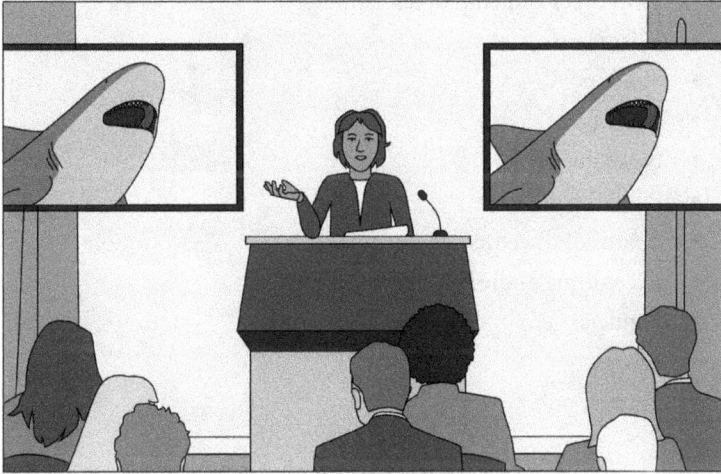

Good communication can make THE difference in a crisis. It's doubly important in a Bull Shark event, a rare circumstance that leads people befuddled and afraid. In any crisis the media is likely to be involved. The media, when it works best, looks strictly for facts in an objective way. Unfortunately, most people fear the mass media thinking that they sensationalize and approach organizations looking for someone to blame and crucify. That is not typically true and, if the organization thinks it is, this may lead to a strongly adversarial situation when it need not. One thing is certain: the media wants the highest-ranking person to step forward and tell the truth (and, if necessary, take the blame).

To communicate effectively, you will need to know your target audiences, the key message you will share with those audiences, ancillary messages, and background materials. You'll also want to pay attention to the timing of your messages and not be bullied by any audience into releasing messages that are ill-timed. Here you will find a list of typical audiences in a crisis.

Target Audiences

For organizations, audiences usually consist of the following:

- Affected parties (injured or having loss of any kind)
- Employees and employees' families
- Clients
- Vendors
- Neighbors
- News media
- Public agencies
- Boards of directors
- Accrediting bodies
- Funders
- Friends
- General public

Key Messages

Again, open and regular communication with all audiences will make your crisis easier to understand and ultimately will help you gain the goodwill of the public. Those audiences need to hear the central message and then hear supplementary messages that appeal to their needs. Typically, the messages look something like these:

- Summary of the incident
- Facts
- Cause of crisis (if known)
- Actions to stabilize the situation
- Time frames
- Acknowledgment of the emotions
- Acceptance of responsibility
- Communication channels being used
- Process for audiences to acquire information

- Depending on the nature of the crisis, messages such as the following may be employed:

Ancillary Messages

You should take every opportunity to tell your story. If your organization has been around for a while, you have had many successes. Remind your audiences of them. Talk about your founding and your founding purpose. Remind your audience of your values.

- Our mission, philosophy, and values
- Our history
- Our staff
- Our procedures
- Our safety record
- Our certifications
- Our inspections
- Our audits
- Our credentials
- Our clients
- Our customers

Background Materials

Most of these messages should have been prepared and be ready to distribute when needed, as well as the following items:

- Fact sheets
- FAQs
- Company profile
- Product/service information
- Quotes from friends/opinion leaders
- Bios
- Access numbers
- Websites

- Q&A documents

Tips for the CEO When Addressing the Media

The CEO must own any crisis and must be the communication source to all audiences, internal and external, when a crisis hits. If the CEO hasn't been trained in public response, she or he must be taught and must practice. This cannot be avoided.

Again, the CEO must speak on behalf of the organization. She or he should have the most credibility and sincerity. As President Harry Truman said (by way of a sign on his desk), "The buck stops here." If the CEO "passes the buck" to someone else, the sincerity of the organization will be questioned along with another spokesperson's authority to make things happen.

Many CEOs are not prepared for this in so far as they lack the experience with the media, lack the confidence to stand before the media (or any audience where they might be questioned), or fear the repercussions of saying the wrong thing. Practicing with the CEO, despite her experience and confidence, is the right approach. When you practice with the CEO, attend to these matters:

IMPRESSION—The CEO must have a serious and confident demeanor and certainly not a "guilty look." This means the CEO must be free to smile when the moment warrants it. The CEO must also be dressed to suit the circumstances. If the event has the CEO getting her hands dirty, she can dress informally, otherwise, she must wear business attire. The same applies to men.

RESPONSE—The CEO must have a "command posture," that is, an upright posture that inhibits leaning or slouching, or otherwise appears unsteady. The CEO must make deep eye contact with the audience, not staring or glaring, but making contact such that all feel they have been noticed. The CEO must have a steady voice with strong volume such that the last person in the gathering can hear the CEO. The best voice has varying tone, pitch, volume, and emphasis. The CEO must avoid fillers (disfluencies such as

"um, ah, er, like, you know" and similar interrupters). These cause
the speaker to seem uncertain at a time when she must be certain
of her message.

MESSAGE—The CEO can read from a prepared script, but it
cannot look or sound like it's being read. The CEO who speaks
from the heart and according to talking points will be received
better. Many CEOs use a strategy of who, what, when, where,
why, how, and how much to guide their remarks. For example, they might say, "You (who) have been the victims of this
catastrophe (what). We now know that on this day (when) too
many lives were lost at the Oregon plant (where). Although
we don't have all the information at this time to assess the
causes (why), we will begin tomorrow to may amends (how)
by dedicating many resources to the cleanup and spending any
amount of money to make this right (how much)."

Some use acronyms. They might use S.U.R.V.I.V.E, that is, "We
have all SEEN (S) what a terrible impact this has had on the community. YOU (U) have had your savings lost and your lives disrupted. No
one could predict the RISK (R) or foreseen what has happened today"
… (and so on acronyms make information processing easier).

Using one of these techniques allows a speaker to seem spontaneous
and not scripted, especially by the legal department.

TIMING—Address the media at your earliest convenience. Make
them partners for information dissemination. Don't hide from
them. Too many crisis communication failures can be attributed to nervous and fearful CEOs who think first about saving
themselves, whereas history has shown that the CEOs who come
forward are more highly regarded when the dust settles, and they
achieve reputations for honesty and doing the right thing at a
time of severe problems.

Q&A—To maintain credibility, the CEO must entertain questions. The first rule is NEVER SPECULATE. Answer questions
truthfully and as fully as possible, give the information you

have. NEVER SAY, "No comment." It's evasive and a cliché for dishonesty. Take questions until the reporters run out of them. Or, you can set a time limit at the beginning of the session remarking that you must attend to aspects of the crisis.

VENUE—You decide where the media conference will be. You decide on the lighting and room temperature, not too hot or cold. You decide on all the physical issues that are within your control.

AUDIOVISUALS—If you use PPT, keep the slides simple. Develop one message per slide. Try to stay under seven words per slide and, above all, use images. We remember images long after we forget words.

THE BEST MEDIA PHILOSOPHY—Be open, honest, and accessible. Give regular briefings. Again, don't lay this off with the PR department. Reporters and their audiences want to see the CEO, the top person, the authority.

Use Storytelling

You will need a story in any event. You will be talking about an inciting event, a cast of characters, rising action, falling action, timing, and falling action.

We have used storytelling from time immemorial since our days in caves. Our brains are wired for stories; much research has proven this, especially the research of Paul Zak whom I suggest you read. We remember stories long after we forget facts and numbers. The best stories help us see the action in our mind's eye.

The media will look for the story of your crisis so you might as well try to manage that story, not by fiction but by responding quickly and honestly to everyone's need to know what happened (and what continues to happen).

Again, telling stories is not about lying or obfuscating but about acknowledging people's need for stories to help them understand.

If you have been struck by a Bull Shark event, you can claim the underdog position. Why not? You ARE the underdog. You were attacked. You were, in many ways, innocent. People love the underdog. They root for the underdog. They want you to win.

You have read about a lost fetus. How does an organization take the underdog role in that situation? It doesn't do it by shutting off communication with an aggrieved mother. It does it by apologizing, admitting error, telling the lawyers to back off, asking for help, bringing the mother (Madonna) close to the CEO, not so that you won't be sued (you should help her anyway with her troubles), but by knowing that someone is hurt and grieving (whether she has had abortions or alcoholism, or committed child abuse, or any misdemeanor). She is a woman whose baby you lost. Period. She is the protagonist. You are the antagonist. Don't be the villain. Do what's right. Don't be evil, as they say.

Will that story have a happy ending? No. It's a tragedy.

CHAPTER 13

What Makes News?

An understanding of the media is crucial when a Bull Shark crisis strikes. Everyone in the organizational hierarchy must understand that it's a bad idea to try to hide from the media or to hide information from them. It's important to understand what makes a good news story. The following list can help you understand. As you look at this list, you will recognize each bullet point and be able to connect a past crisis to each item. In any event, the media likes:

- Something new
- Catastrophe
- Human interest
- Sports
- Health care
- Money
- Cute (kids and animals)

- Religion
- Heroism
- Celebrity
- Politics
- Crime
- "If it bleeds, it leads."

When you know what interests the media, you can recognize your situation. The media are interested in the items in that list because their viewers have those interests. We have a morbid curiosity to view catastrophe, a great need to feel safe from crime, a social need to know what others are doing, especially the rich and famous. Sports fascinates us and politics puzzles us. Our brains are wired to notice and pay attention to anything new. When we know these things about ourselves and the media, we can understand better how to work with the media and the public.

The media want to understand so that they can translate events for their readers/viewers. The media want to be seen as accurate and objective. The more accuracy you can give them, the more likely they are to be objective.

Media relations begin long before any crisis. If you have no relations with the media, you are an unknown quantity to them and you begin on fair footing. If you have had an antagonistic relationship with them, that relationship is likely to continue. If you have an open, honest, and accessible relationship with them, that will serve you both well. It won't get you any special treatment or favors but it will bias the media, initially, to your favor, that is they will believe you, at first.

I always developed an open and honest relationship with the media. At times, I told certain media facts about my organization that the organization would rather have had me not tell anyone. My relationship was such that one reporter who won a Pulitzer Prize asked if he could "hide" in my office until the furor died down. I'd say that showed a good relationship with that reporter.

Know How to Work With the Media

Working with the media doesn't require any specialized knowledge. If you want the media to partner with you, do these simple things:

- Be credible
- Be useful
- Be selective
- Be simple
- Be in control
- Be objective
- Be realistic

When you have been credible with the media, you are likely to gain their trust. If they don't trust you, the game is lost. They will circle around you to get their information elsewhere.

If you want their cooperation, you can find ways to be useful to them. This doesn't start the day of the crisis, by the way. You need to develop these ways with the media from day one as an organization. I built a reputation of honesty and usefulness with the media, and it served me well for years. If I saw a particularly great photo opportunity, I called news photographers and tipped them to the photo op. If I could get them access to an otherwise off-limits scenario, I'd get it. They are a very competitive and ambitious group and if you can help them get a scoop, they appreciate it.

You can't be everything to everyone and you need to select carefully the information you're going to disperse. Bottom line: don't let your years of success and good purpose get lost in other messages.

Always keep your messages simple—use action verbs, active voice, and write and speak with short words, short sentences, and short paragraphs. Remember that most of your audience have a reading level of eighth grade. They're not stupid; they just haven't focused on public speaking and writing the way you have, especially your PR team.

Be objective and realistic. Don't expect that what you say is always correct or that everyone wants to hear things from your point of view. They don't. Audiences are motivated by self-interest. Everyone is motivated by self-interest. Stay in control. Know that you're in a very high emotional situation, but understand and control your emotions. Know the emotions of others. This is being empathetic, or emotionally intelligent.

Know How to Act With the Media

Among the audiences you must consider is the media. You want them to treat you fairly and accurately. Try to follow these tips to achieve that:

- Be in command.
- Know the facts; repeat them.
- Correct inaccuracies.
- Consider a question as an opportunity.
- Appear human and concerned.
- Stay loose.
- Tell the truth.

Let's begin at the end. Tell the truth, no matter how it might hurt. If you lie or exaggerate, you will be found out. In a crisis, especially a Bull Shark event, you can be the aggrieved party, or you can be the target. You didn't ask for this. It was so unexpected that few could have been prepared. You can be the underdog one minute and the villain the next. Sympathy can be with you or anger against you. Don't ask for pity, as the CEO of British Petroleum (BP) did when he said he wanted his "life back." Unless someone in your organization has physically harmed others, you can be seen as a victim. But, don't play the victim.

Telling the truth actually helps to keep you in command. When you know the facts, you are in command. When you know them and repeat them, you stay in control. You will certainly want to correct inaccuracies and if you think about questions as opportunities, instead of attempts to trap you, your approach will be better.

Above all, be a human, talking to other humans, and being concerned about people. We are a social species; it's the reason for our success. Show your concern for others, not just yourself and your organization.

Some Media Tips

A poet said that we forget what speakers say, but we always remember the way they make us feel. That's an absolute truth. What do you remember from your high school graduation speech? Your college graduation speech? Probably little. Perhaps a bit of advice or a joke. The truth is that people forget what they hear, most of it, in a very short time after they've heard it. They also remember an impression of you. Did you slouch, stutter, shift? Did you use fillers and sound uncertain? Did your clothes hang on you? Did you flinch when asked critical questions?

https://quoteinvestigator.com/2014/04/06/they-feel/

- Be Alert! Be aware of body language.
- Be enthusiastic (if appropriate). Be sorry. Be sympathetic. Be something.
- Remember that how you look is as important as what you say.
- Remember that most questions are generated by the answers you give.
- Dress right for TV. Wear no loud ties, finely striped shirts, small checks, black or white, no reds, no leather, no light-sensitive glasses.
- If you get "dry mouth," bite the tip of your tongue!
- If you become anxious, relax your muscles. Breathe more deeply. Count your breaths.

You really need to have someone watch your body language and tell you what your body is saying, particularly if your body language is at odds with your spoken language. Were your arms crossed on your chest (protecting your heart)? Was your head tucked into your shirt like a turtle hiding from a predator? Did you shake your head back and forth (a "yes" gesture) when you were saying that you didn't do something (President Clinton did this when he said he "did not have sex with that woman")? Were you making any micro gestures, those telltale expressions that are hardly visible to conscious examination but slip into the unconscious minds of audiences, a brief smirk, perhaps.

Be aware, also, of how you look, especially on TV/video. You can maintain control over this as well as the setting where you are interviewed. If you are not dressed for the occasion, excuse yourself and go change. The others can wait. If they try to videotape/photograph you at a bad angle or with bad lighting, move to a better location. For instance, you don't want the light coming from directly below your face (the "devil look"), or directly above your head, the look of hollow eye sockets and fatigue. Take control or put your trust in an aide who is informed of these subtleties and can make the arrangements of you.

The "Do Not Do" List

The following list is simple but critical. You should be able to remember these important no–no's.

- Do NOT speculate.
- Do NOT say, "No Comment."
- Do NOT use jargon or "biz speak."
- Do NOT ramble.
- Do NOT make undeliverable promises.
- Do NOT argue or justify.

Do not provide opinions, just facts. Don't try to guess what happened or what the results might be. At the same time, never say, "No comment." It just suggests, very strongly, that you have something to hide and that you are insensitive to everyone and their problems. Avoid jargon at all costs. Use simple, plain language. Warren Buffett, a man who knows a lot of financial jargon, says that when he's giving a presentation he pretends he's talking to his sisters. Don't ramble. Use short crisp answers. Answer authentically. Don't make any promises unless you say that you vow to help everyone injured in any way to get their lives back together. Lastly, never argue with anyone. Stay cool. Keep a clear head.

CHAPTER 14

Handle Social Media

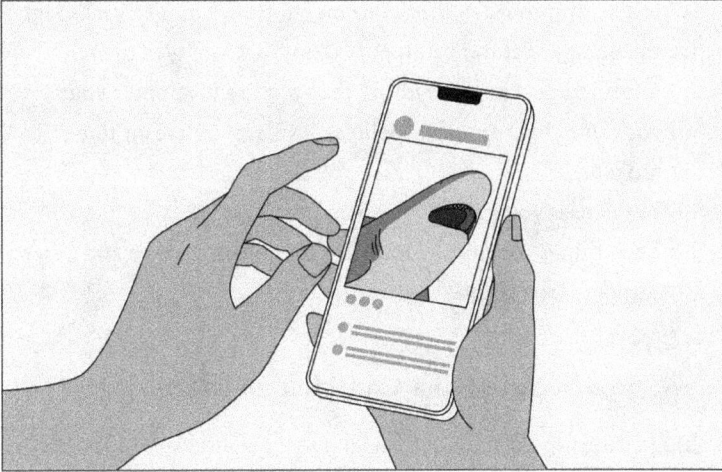

The word of your BULL SHARK ATTACK will reach the world through social media before you address the media. Rumors will circulate, misinformation will be rampant, accusations will fly. Stay calm through all of this. Tell the truth of what you know and understand that people of low ethical standards, especially those with whom you've had differences, philosophical and otherwise, will try to trash you and your organization. Stay tough. Do these things:

1. Appoint someone to oversee your social media, specifically the crisis comments, and gather information about the tenure of the chat.
2. Respond ASAP.
3. Go for authenticity and transparency.

4. Use social media to circulate your messages—use brief and succinct messages that use short words, short sentences, and short paragraphs.

5. Empathize.

6. Use video when you can; it's more effective than text.

7. Expect to be trashed; social media thrives on negativity.

8. Don't get into a pissing contest with anyone.

9. Hire a firm to listen for brand mentions; it's money well spent.

10. Encourage staff to post; they will anyway, and give them information, FAQs, anything they can use to support your position. Don't give the "policies." Rules were meant to be broken.

11. Evaluate as you go; adjust as you must.

12. Keep things "organic." Don't fuss about brand voice and other corporate confusion. Update regularly.

Social Media Can Help or Harm

In 2009, early in the days of social media, United Airlines baggage handlers were seen throwing guitar cases at Chicago's O'Hare International Airport. When musician Dave Carroll arrived at his location, he found his $3,500 Taylor guitar broken. He said that he spoke to three United employees who treated him with disregard and disrespect. He filed a claim with United Airlines and they told him he was ineligible because he failed to file the claim in time.

Carroll got his revenge by posting a YouTube video of a scathing song he had created about the incident. It had 150,000 views the first day. It soon had half a million views and within two years it had over 11 million views. As of this writing, it has garnered over 22 million views. To say it went viral is a huge understatement.

The traditional media caught on to the story and soon United Airlines was begging Carroll, apologizing to him and asking to use his video for "training purposes."

As usually happens, organizations peripherally connected to the incident saw PR value. For instance, the owner of Taylor Guitars offered Carroll two guitars for free. Carroll's song hit number one on the iTunes

Music Store the week after its release, and Carroll parlayed the simple incident into a speaking career.

https://en.wikipedia.org/wiki/United_Breaks_Guitars.

A Bull Shark Event?

Probably not. If United is testing its vulnerabilities, it should expect someone to be very unhappy about the way their luggage is mishandled, and they should have plans in place to deal with it. But, if you consider the year and the relative newness of social media, perhaps no one would have thought of an online virus that could destroy the reputation of an airline. That would make it a Bull Shark event, for sure.

Navigate Social Media Properly During a Crisis

In times of crisis, social media becomes a powerful tool for communication, connection, and support. Whether you're a business, organization, or individual, understanding how to effectively use social media during challenging situations is crucial. Let's dive into some key strategies:

1. Know Your Audience

Before posting anything, identify the audience you want to reach. Are you speaking to internal stakeholders, external customers, or both? Tailor your messages accordingly. Consider addressing your audience by name to create a more personal connection.

2. Listen to Your Audience

Social media is a two-way street. Listen to what your customers are saying. Monitor hashtags and keywords they use. Understand their needs and focus on sharing essential information. Avoid tone-deaf messaging by being empathetic and responsive.

3. Plan Ahead

While the future may be uncertain, planning is essential. Outline an evergreen content schedule for the next 30, 60, and 90 days. Having a plan ensures you won't scramble for content at the last minute. Share quality messages that resonate with your audience.

4. Show Empathy and Build Trust

Remember that your customers are dealing with a crisis too. Acknowledge the challenges they face. Share messages that demonstrate empathy and understanding. Building trust during difficult times will strengthen your brand's reputation.

5. Create a Crisis Communication Policy

Create a social media crisis communication policy. This document should outline steps to take during a crisis, including pausing scheduled posts, assessing impact, formulating timely responses, and addressing the problem. Having a clear policy ensures consistency and preparedness.

6. Use Different Formats

Consider using live broadcasts or prerecorded videos to convey important messages. Additionally, provide links to long-form responses on your official website. If possible, set up a "dark site" for crisis-specific information.

Remember, social media is a valuable tool for connecting with your audience during a crisis. Use it wisely, show empathy, and provide relevant information. Together, we can navigate challenging times effectively.

The Boeing 737 Max Crisis

Boeing has had its share of crises and by now should know the drill. But, there's always something that isn't there. Again, we can debate whether their last debacle is a Black Swan, a Gray Rhino, or a Bull Shark. I would say Bull Shark, but surely someone at Boeing must have considered that part of the wall of a new 737 Max 9 aircraft might blow off. I know, it's hard to think that way, but as the bumper sticker so astutely counsels everyone, "Sh*t Happens."

This time it happened with an Alaska Airlines flight with 177 people on board. After it took off from Portland, Oregon, it made an emergency landing because of a sizeable hole on the side of the plane.

Thank God, no one was killed or crippled, but, as you can expect video clips of the incident went viral quickly.

When he was interviewed by the media, Boeing CEO Dave Calhoun said he was "devastated" and "emotional" after seeing videos from the Alaska Airlines mid-flight blowout.

Calhoun acknowledged to CNBC that "What happened is exactly what you saw, a fuselage plug blew out. That's the mistake, it can never happen." He also said that the company is working with the government to inspect every one of their airplanes to make sure that they're "in conformance with our design, which is a proven design."

Let's Take a Look at This Crisis and the Boeing Response

1. Boeing responded quickly. That's a good thing.
2. Boeing's CEO took the spotlight; that's a good thing.
3. Calhoun sounded transparent, to a point. He used some bullsh*t in his remarks, a "quality escape occurred?" Really? Passive voice? Jargon? He said he would be sharing more information as their review of the planes took place, adding, "I'm confident that that process will not only prevent an accident, but maybe more importantly, the data we collect from each and every one of those inspections, the data we collect will inform all of the actions that we have to take as a company." That's a good thing.
4. Calhoun spoke to his staff. He said, "We're going to approach this number one acknowledging our mistake." That's a good thing.
5. Calhoun promised to be transparent and work with outside agencies. He said, "We're going to approach it with 100 percent and complete transparency every step of the way. We are going to work with the NTSB that is investigating the accident itself to find out what the cause is."

6. He didn't pass the buck by laying the blame squarely at the feet of aviation supplier Spirit AeroSystems. He said that he is confident in their CEO Patrick Shanahan. "We're not going to point fingers there. Because yes, it escaped their factory, but then it escaped ours too," he said. "So we're all in this together. We have to figure this one out." That's a good thing.

7. He looked and sounded like a leader; that's a good thing.

8. Employees had some negative comments. One said that the jet was "designed by clowns, who in turn are supervised by monkeys." That hurts; it really hurts.

9. Calhoun appealed to parental instincts when he said, "When I got that picture, all I could think about ... I've got kids, I've got grandkids, and so do you. This stuff matters. Every detail matters." That was a good thing.

10. Pieces of the airplane keep showing up in people's yards. It's highly visual and keeps the event in the news. That's a very bad thing.

Things didn't get any better for Boeing. The Federal Aviation Administration (FAA) ordered many Boeing 737 Max 9 aircrafts to be temporarily grounded so that investigators could try to determine what had happened. That, of course, messed with the plans of many people as flights were canceled left and right.

Greatly affected was Alaska Airlines. United Airlines canceled over 150 flights. Both airlines apologized profusely and promised to get flights scheduled again. But, the FAA had other plans. The chairperson of the NTSB said that she had a lot of questions for Calhoun. "He stated that mistakes were made, and I'd like to understand what mistakes he is referring to," she told the media.

As often happens in situations like this, politicians got involved. President Biden was said to be "monitoring the situation" and a lawmaker from Ohio who sat on the Senate Commerce Committee wanted to start hearings to determine what was going on.

The event wasn't likely to go away soon because a preliminary report wasn't expected to be released for three to four weeks.

All told, it was a bad month for Boeing, Alaska Airlines, and United Airlines. Anyone who visited Boeing's website would have seen this:

About the Boeing 737 MAX

The 737 MAX delivers enhanced efficiency, improved environmental performance, and increased passenger comfort to the single-aisle market. Incorporating advanced technology winglets and efficient engines, the 737 MAX offers excellent economics, reducing fuel use and emissions by 20 percent while producing a 50 percent smaller noise footprint than the airplanes it replaces. Additionally, 737 MAX offers up to 14 percent lower airframe maintenance costs than the competition. Passengers will enjoy the Boeing Sky Interior, highlighted by modern sculpted sidewalls and window reveals, LED lighting that enhances the sense of spaciousness and larger pivoting overhead storage bins.

When your Bull Shark bites, remember to review your content. It may hold you up to ridicule.

https://en.wikipedia.org/wiki/Boeing_737_MAX_groundings.

CHAPTER 15

Consider the Differences in Cultures With Multicultural Companies

Most large corporations, of course, have offices in many countries, which will make managing a crisis much more difficult.

Communicating cross-culturally is difficult in the best of circumstances. When distance and timing are added, communication can seem impossible. For you it's 3 p.m., but for them it's 3 a.m. They may respond quickly, but others may take time to think about a response. Contexts certainly differ. For cultures that communicate inductively, those that communicate deductively can seem accusatory. Some cultures are slow to express blame, if they express it at all. Perhaps most troubling is that some cultures disagree openly, whereas some would never agree with a supervisor or executive.

To manage a global crisis, follow these suggestions:

1. Communication will need to be used in either low or high context, but not both.
2. Leadership must demand that a western or eastern approach to all considerations be employed, including feedback, authority, evaluation, decision making, and persuading. Local laws will need to apply, and local politics must be understood.
3. Experts will need to be consulted and contracted with.
4. Schedules will need to be rigid and accommodating to all parties.
5. Media management will need to accommodate time zones and audience interests.

https://en.wikipedia.org/wiki/High-context_and_low-context_cultures.

CHAPTER 16

Can You Use AI in a Crisis?

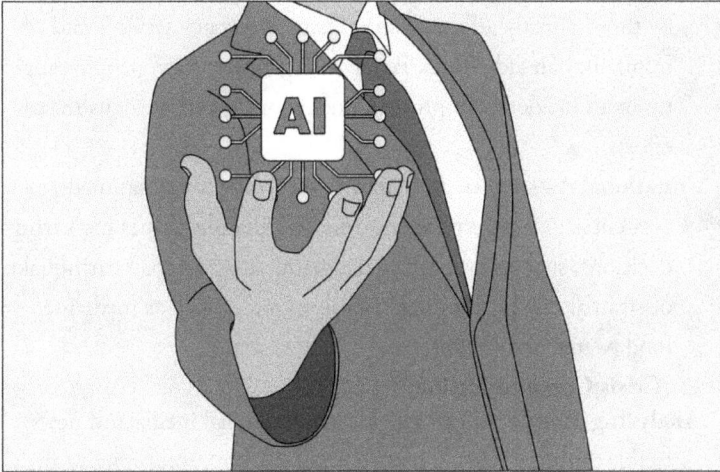

Of course, you can. And, of course you should. Artificial intelligence (AI) has changed the game in every discipline and expectation. Tools such as ChatGPT can help you anticipate, simulate, estimate, calculate, facilitate, and communicate, among other things.

First, Bull Shark thinking is required before a crisis. As this book has said, you must anticipate the un-anticipate-able. You can feed AI crisis scenarios and ask AI to find similar scenarios that may affect your organization. Then, you can feed AI information to help you to simulate a Bull Shark event and plan for such events. AI can help you estimate costs and facilitate actions. Lastly, and very importantly, it will help you develop communications.

Rapid and accurate communication is critical in any crisis. AI can create messages for you in minutes. Of course, as has been said about any technology, "Garbage in, garbage out." You must refine the demands you ask of AI. Without question, AI will save you time and money, when used correctly.

During a crisis, AI can play a crucial role in various ways:

1. **Situational Awareness and Emergency Response:**

Social Media Data Analysis: AI tools can extract critical information from social media channels such as Twitter. While most tweets contain noncritical information, during crises, data shared by those directly affected can inform emergency services and humanitarian aid efforts. For instance, tweets from people caught up in an incident can provide clues about where to focus rescue efforts.

Situational Awareness: AI helps provide real-time situational awareness to first responders. This information shapes life-saving decisions, such as evacuating dangerous areas after an earthquake or strategically positioning critical resources such as medicine, food, water, and shelter.

2. **Crisis Communication:**

Analyzing Trends: AI can quickly analyze social media and news trends during a crisis. Crisis communication professionals can use AI to identify potential risks and develop targeted response strategies.

3. **Disaster Resilience and Relief:**

Prediction and Projection: AI aids in predicting and projecting natural disasters, helping authorities prepare and respond effectively.

Monitoring and Early Detection: AI tools monitor events in real time and detect potential new risks.

Data Sharing: Platforms such as Facebook share anonymized data about people's movements and population density maps to forecast virus spread. Google search data has also been used to track infectious diseases.

4. **Fighting Misinformation:**

AI helps combat misinformation by safeguarding users from phishing, conspiracy theories, and false claims. Platforms such as Google and YouTube provide accurate information and remove misleading content.

Remember that while AI offers immense potential, collaboration and trust-building are essential to maximize its benefits during crises.

Some Rules of Usage

Above all, use common, simple language. Avoid jargon and technical language. Address an eighth-grade reading level a common language. When writing, use these tactics:

1. Prefer action verbs: Avoid abstractions and being verbs. Audiences will want to know what you did and what you intend to do to remedy your failures.
2. Prefer active voice: Active voice reveals responsibility. Passive voice disguises it. Don't use sentences—in writing or in speaking —that sound like this, "The implementation of the project was miscalculated due to the replication of certain inefficiencies." That is passive voice creating bullshit.
3. Use people as subjects of your communication: Again, if you say or write the previous sentence ("The implementation of the project was miscalculated due to the replication of certain inefficiencies"), you have placed np persons in a place of responsibility.
4. Write and speak with logic: Take the time to think about the logic of what you're saying. In that regard, write paragraphs that have a topic sentence and then repeat them in your presentations.
5. Keep transitions clear: Don't jump from one topic to another without transitioning smoothly.
6. Use metaphor, simile, and analogy: You can help your audience understand what happened by using these literary devices.

More than anything, keep everything simple. Use short words, short sentences, and short paragraphs. Da Vinci said, "Simplicity is the ultimate sophistication." It is. Einstein said, in effect, that if you can't explain something with simplicity you don't understand it well enough. Steve Jobs was an acolyte of simplicity, hence the designs of the Mac, iPad, iPhone, and other Apple products. In a crisis, overcommunicate. Hold media briefings often during the first days of the crisis. Hold them every day as the crisis unfolds and new information is available.

Use the CEO as spokesperson, as has already been noted, and then choose well-spoken subject matter experts to address specific topics, especially technical matters and increase tension among all parties, both internal and external. Of course, open and respectful communication doesn't begin when a Bull Shark attacks. The organizations that fare best in a crisis are those that have been openly and honestly communicating with their many audiences long before a crisis happens.

A lack of communication will deepen distrust and tension. Determine to communicate and to be cited for being great communicators after the crisis has resolved. Also, determine to be seen as having been: compassionate, collaborative, and credible.

We shouldn't have to say that we are humans trying to communicate with other humans and to recognize that we are emotional beings who think, as opposed to thinking beings who emote. You will experience few moments in your life when emotions run higher than in a crisis. You will need all the emotional intelligence you can muster, empathy being the foremost. Show your compassion. Show that you suffer with all of the victims of the crisis.

Show that you are willing to listen. This has been called the most important executive skill for a reason. People feel valued when you listen to them. Don't talk so much. Ask questions. Gather information. Do this, of course, before and after a crisis. Collaboration and listening will help you learn.

Ultimately, you want to be credible. You want audiences to perceive you as honest and competent. This means being available and visible. When the World Trade Center was destroyed by terrorists on 9/11, Rudy Guiliani stood in the midst of the destruction and reassured New York City that the towers would rise again. He has done much good in his life and career and some bad, but he will always live in the minds of New Yorkers for his moment at Ground Zero.

CHAPTER 17

Can Humor Be Used to Defuse a Crisis?

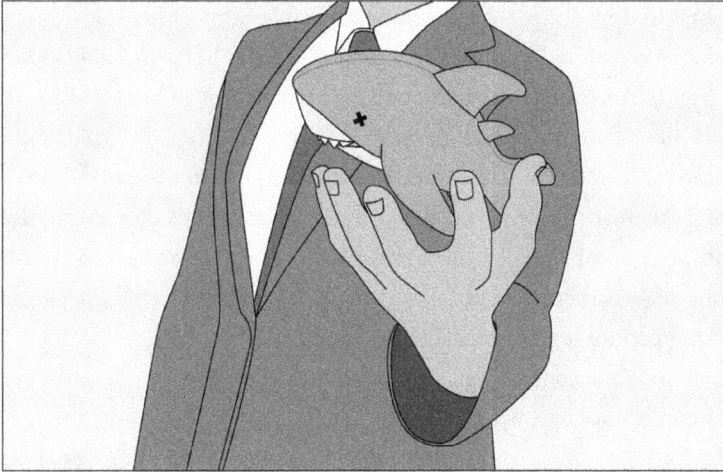

Ask K. In 2018, KFC experienced a Bull Shark event; it ran out of chicken across the United Kingdom and Ireland. That was unthinkable, right? Who would have ever dreamed that a famous company acclaimed for its namesake product, chicken, would not have been able to deliver on its "Finger-Licking Good" promise. Some Bull Shark thinking could have surely surfaced that possibility.

In any event, what did KFC and its creative agency dream up as a reaction to the problem? They used humor. They created an ad that featured an empty bucket of chicken with the large letters of KFC transposed to FCK! The public loved it! KFC effectively acknowledged their failure, took ownership of it, and apologized in the coolest way by saying, "FCK!" Of course, everyone knew what the transposed acronym stood for, and everyone was quick to laugh and forgive.

Obviously, for an organization to use humor as a response to a crisis, the crisis needs to be humor-worthy. An Exxon Valdez crisis is not going to lend itself to humor, nor a Bhopal, nor a 9/11, and certainly not a lost fetus.

www.wired.com/story/kfc-chicken-crisis-shortage-supply-chain-logistics-experts/

A Crisis Is an Emotional Powder Keg

It has been said that we are emotional beings who think, not thinking beings who emote. That tells us that we are likely to be led by our emotions in a crisis. And, the primary emotion that will drive us will be FEAR.

Our brains are wired to keep us alive, to help us make quick decisions in the face of danger. We have a part of our brain called the amygdala that, together with other brain areas, help us defend ourselves and prepare for battle. Unfortunately, we are sometimes too driven by these brain structures and fall victim to "amygdala hijack" wherein we cannot control our emotional responses.

A primary control function of our brain resides in the prefrontal cortex. We need to use that part of our brains to overcome amygdala hijack. That doesn't mean that we should put all emotions on hold, however. We especially need emotional intelligence at a time of crisis. We need to understand our emotions and know how to control them. We need to understand the emotions of others. They may have anger, fear, sadness, or disgust. These emotions will not feel good to us, but we must acknowledge and value them.

We can take a first step to understanding others by listening to them. This means not being defensive or deferring to legalities. It means not debating them about right and wrong. It means active listening techniques such as self-disclosure, paraphrasing, and using support language such as, "It sounds as if you are very angry."

We can take another step forward by building a relationship with others by saying, "We're in this together," especially if you indeed are. You can use techniques that hostage negotiators use such as, "Help me understand" and "Talk to me." Remember, those who are angry want to be heard. Encourage dialogue, listen deeply, record what's being said, and examine all suggestions, even those that are said in a vengeful and threatening manner.

Sixty-Nine Percent of Businesses Are "Smoldering"

"Given the severity and the frequency of major crises, what keeps us from preparing better? Denial! Far too many organizations have the attitude that it can't and won't happen to them. It will.

"Research shows that better prepared organizations experience significantly fewer crises and are significantly more profitable. The moral: Crisis management is not only the right thing to do, it is good for business."

Marshall Goldsmith, HBR

https://hbr.org/2008/09/preparing-your-company-for-a-crisis

Remember

By now, in this book, you should understand that the way you communicate can make or break your crisis response. That said, remember these things:

1. Public perception is formed by emotion, not reason.
2. Eighty percent of disasters are people-generated and can be avoided.
   www.prb.org/resources/disaster-risk/
3. Thirty-one percent of business crises are "sudden."
4. Absence equals uncaring.
5. The reality is that we are living in a world defined by social consciousness.
6. Nothing, remember this, nothing is "off-the-record." What you say can and may be held against you. Be honest but be sensible.

More Communication Issues to Consider

How Will You Respond to a Crisis in a Hybrid Working Environment?

It's no secret that the world of work has changed drastically since the COVID-19 pandemic. Many workers have not returned to the office and that will create what might be called "a hybrid crisis response." What will that entail?

1. Staff will learn about the crisis at different intervals.
2. Some staff will be in office, some at home, some at Starbucks, some on a boat.
3. Leaders will struggle to coordinate people and their roles and obligations.
4. Communication will be nightmarish.
5. Staff will exist by Zoom with its special strengths and weaknesses (no body language, failing internet connections, myriad distractions, etc.).
6. Teamwork will be challenged.
7. Collaboration and the sharing of ideas and approaches will be limited.
8. Continuity will suffer.

What can be done about this?

1. Leaders must demand a central meeting place for managing the crisis.
2. The crisis team must lead these efforts; the crisis support team must engage.
3. Leaders must communicate quickly.
4. Messages must be simple following the KISS principle.
5. Messages must be targeted.
6. Messages must be brief.
7. Messages must repeat themes.
8. Messages must be timely.
9. Messages must be honest.
10. Messages must use appropriate media.
11. Messages must have power.

CHAPTER 18

Recovery—What Do We Do Now?

So, the crisis hit and took everyone by surprise. The executives scrambled to control the situation. The media acted responsibly, reporting on every nuance as the crisis unfolded. Few people were injured, and some equipment and materials were damaged. Lawsuits were begun. Executives met with boards to review the situation. Time, that heals all wounds, passed. The recovery process had to begin.

How Does an Organization Recover From a Major Crisis?

Well, if you're Johnson & Johnson, you land on your feet doing better than you had before the crisis. This happened, not because you expected someone to poison people by putting cyanide inside your pain relief capsules but because you followed your mission and values.

Additionally, you were open, honest, and accessible to all parties. You told the truth, you cooperated with the media, the government, the police, the FBI. In the end, you regained market share and sales of your product and you continued to be voted the most trusted company in the United States. Or, as has been said more graphically, "You fell in sh*t and came out smelling like a rose."

Your crisis has ended. The media has departed. Staff are insecure. The brand is beleaguered. A general malaise has settled throughout the entire organization. What now? What shall we do to win back trust from all audiences? How do we get back to normal? What is normal? Will we ever be the same as we were?

Communicate Aggressively

No tactic is as important in a crisis as open, honest, and accurate communication. It serves as the keystone to good crisis management and is reflected in many parts of this document. A good plan will have prepared you with a list of target audiences. Some will require more urgent attention than others, but they are all important. Some need personal attention and some will gain information through more common channels, such as the mass media and social media.

Admit Your Mistakes

Use every means at your disposal to communicate the most important messages to all of your audiences and do it with all of the media at your disposal. Whether or not you were at fault, you are well served to apologize. This is especially true of your harshest critics. The saying says, "You can't win in a pissing contest with a skunk." Don't try. Use a jitsu approach and bend with their blows. Acknowledge their claims, unless they are totally contrived and factually untrue.

Fix Your Own House

The damage has been done. Your employees are insecure. Your customers have run off. Your board has lost faith. It's time to fix the broken brand.

This could be the best time to use paid media to remind the public that you have a history of doing good things (if you do) and that your mission and values are directed toward serving the community. (You might want to visit this point well in advance of any potential crisis.) Communicate rigorously with your most important audiences and pay special attention to your employees and customers. Review your processes and protocols for errors or oversights that the crisis made visible. Create crisis prevention activities and appoint people to oversee them. Practice. Run drills. Brainstorm. Plan for every eventuality. Bottom line: Invest in these activities because they will ultimately save you money.

Learn From Your Mistakes

If you were unable to anticipate the crisis and got caught, as they say, with your pants down, you need to take stock of the situation and find the gold in the rubble. Ask yourself these questions:

- What did we do wrong that led to the crisis?
- Who were the players who should have seen it coming? Why didn't they see it? If they sensed it, why didn't they speak up?
- What can we do to prevent another crisis?
- How does our experience in the crisis prepare us for the future?
  - What did we do right?
  - What did we do wrong?
  - Who made the right decisions? The wrong decisions?
- Where are we most vulnerable going forward?
- How are we organized to prevent future crises?
- What should we budget for crisis prevention and preparedness?
- Where should we house responsibility for crisis anticipation and management?

Jump-Start Your Planning

If you had a bad experience in your crisis, you likely had no crisis plan. Not every crisis can be anticipated, especially the Bull Shark events. As we said, they arise out of nowhere. But, EVERY organization—from one employee to 100,000 employees—can expect a crisis. The best way to manage a crisis is, obviously, to be prepared for it, to literally have off-the-shelf plans in place, like fire extinguishers in a glass case to be pulled out and used on the crisis.

Hire a Third Party

Any executive in any organization is too much in the trees to see the forest. CEOs don't see vulnerabilities and, in fact, aren't typically looking for them. When you deal every day with organizational matters of marketing and product development, finances, HR, learning and development, and all of the other important internal matters, it's hard to extract yourself to see above the tedium at potential problems—in fact, you don't want to see problems. You have your eye on the horizon, the future.

Your best approach is to hire a crisis consultant, someone who has been there and experienced the effects of different crises, someone who can unearth vulnerabilities. It's not unlike hiring an expert to "child-proof" your home, someone who can come to your house and help you find the potential dangers to toddlers—sharp-edged corners, easy-to-reach electrical outlets, accessible stairwells and windows, and all the rest of the places we never think of when we're busy raising children and marveling at their innocence and beauty.

An experienced crisis consultant can help you see what you don't see, which may be right in front of you. The consultant can also help generate potential problems by interviewing staff who may not feel comfortable talking to their supervisor. A consultant can gain trust and promise anonymity by asking questions that superiors may not think to ask. "What makes your job risky? What potential failures do you see in the equipment or facilities? Do you see any hazards that might affect customers or visitors? If you were going to redesign the work process to make it safer, what would you do?" These questions and more should be asked routinely, anyway. But, everyone is busy doing his or her job, and, in fact, usually made to focus on their goals to the exemption of creative thinking and assessing crisis vulnerabilities. Think of the last time you were at work, and someone asked you to assess vulnerabilities of any kind. Again, a consultant who is chosen for their knowledge of crisis/facilitation/strategic planning will serve you well at a fraction of the cost you will incur had experienced a crisis.

Review

You've read about the crises this author was involved in and you've heard the steps that you can take to avoid being attacked by a Bull Shark event. Having gone through corporate crises, I have identified steps that now seem second nature, and obvious, to me. I can't imagine why every organization wouldn't take these steps and regularly review them. It's not like they're difficult. To protect yourself and your organization, you only need to schedule some time to brainstorm and then ask staff to put together materials that can be brought to bear in the event of a crisis.

What kind of materials might a hospital have prepared to circulate? Think about it: How many babies are born and nurtured in your hospital every year? How many have been born and safely handled from your beginnings? How many physicians practice at your organization? What are their credentials? How many safe flights does your airline land every week? How many people have safely used your product every day? You need these kinds of materials to put your crisis in context where it belongs.

Put the Crisis in Context

A crisis doesn't happen in a vacuum. Your company has been around for 10 years, 50 years, 100 years. In that time, you have safely served hundreds of clients, thousands of clients, millions of clients.

You have success stories of the lives you have made better, the lives you have saved, perhaps. Have those facts and figures available to pull out at a moment's notice and use them. Single events happen, but they happen in context. Don't let anyone keep the focus on the immediate situation.

All Face Crises. Few Face Bull Sharks

Crises cannot be avoided. No organization has complete control over fate. But, you can manage a crisis when you anticipate one and are prepared to respond. That means you must follow these steps:

1. IDENTIFY YOUR VULNERABILITIES

   DO THIS FIRST. Every organization has vulnerabilities. Hospitals lose babies, have surgeons infected with COVID. Banks overextend themselves, have employees who commit fraud. Universities have cheating scandals, free speech issues, suicides. Identify your WEAK SPOTS. But, moreover, look for your Bull Sharks. They are not just rare, they are UNTHINKABLE. Take the time to go deep into your collective imagination to surface these beasts. Then plan the ways you will handle them.

2. IDENTIFY YOUR CRISIS TEAM

   Do yourself a favor. Keep the team SMALL. Who should belong? The CEO, the COO, the corporate counsel, the CMO, and the security chief. They can make broad decisions. Too many chefs spoil the broth. An unwieldy group can make quick decisions and response impossible.

3. APPOINT A SPOKESPERSON

   Appoint the CEO. Anyone else is NOT the final authority. COACH this person, if need be, in the ways to deal with the media. Practice. Videotape the CEO.

4. CREATE A CRISIS SUPPORT TEAM

   Pick RELIABLE PEOPLE. This group will manage many of the crisis DETAILS and deliver much of the crisis SUPPORT MATERIAL. HR belongs on this team, along with people from finance, customer relations, as well as subject matter experts and social media specialists.

5. CREATE A PLAN FOR EACH OF YOUR MOST LIKELY CRISES

   This is a laborious task, but it will help immensely in the event of a crisis. The plan will include many IMPORTANT DETAILS: team meeting rooms, team members' phone numbers and other contact information, FAQs about the organization, relevant statistics, a media room with computers, telephones, refreshments, podium, and other essentials. Keep these plans handy and be ready to implement them. RUN A DRILL. You can call it a "DRY RUN" or "maneuvers"; call it anything, but do it. PRACTICE ... Practice ... Practice. Know where everyone goes, what they do when they get there, and what they say, if anything.

6. STUDY PAST CRISES

   Use the TYLENOL CRISIS as your guide. That crisis will tell you to BE OPEN, HONEST, and ACCESSIBLE. TYLENOL will tell you to DEFER to the public and its safety and concerns, and to defer to your mission and philosophy. The Tylenol Crisis will also encourage you to IGNORE the financial concerns. Johnson & Johnson lost millions of dollars and all market share. But, they gained it back because of their attitude and behavior.

7. EXPECT ANYTHING TO HAPPEN

   The bumper sticker says, "SH*T HAPPENS!" It does, when you LEAST EXPECT IT, at the MOST INCONVENIENT times. But, if you manage crises BEFORE THEY HAPPEN, you will manage them a lot better WHEN they happen!

8. COMMUNICATE CONSTANTLY

   With the media, always:

   1. Provide clear facts.
   2. Be concise, cohesive, and coherent.
   3. Inspire confidence.
   4. Be inoffensive.
   5. Avoid accusations.
   6. Apologize profusely.
   7. Stay calm and respectful.
   8. Escort the media to your CEO.
   9. Prepare supplemental materials.
   10. Build relationships based on truth and trust.

   Keep the public informed:

   1. Interact with the outside world (don't shut yourself off).
   2. Have regular updates, even if you're repeating vital information.

3. Think of your employees as an important "public."

4. Control your security team. You need security but not bull dogs.

9. CHOOSE THE BEST CRISIS TEAM

Keep it small and manageable. Include these people:

CEO, CMO, LEGAL, COO, CFO—Don't let anyone dominate the conversation; the quiet person might have the best idea.

10. CHOOSE THE BEST CRISIS SUPPORT TEAM

Put security on this team, along with the PR people, the in-house printers/copiers, writers, photographers, food service manager, customer service rep, tech people, and social media experts. Keep the group focused and agile.

Remember the words of Winston Churchill: "Never let a good crisis go to waste." Learn from this crisis to respond better to the next one. Look for the opportunities that every crisis presents. Good luck!

About the Author

Edward Barr is a business expert who has worked in corporate communications and marketing for over 20 years and has dealt with several "Bull Shark events" as described in this book. His way of telling stories about those events is engaging and illuminating. Also, his methods for identifying, avoiding, and dealing with crises will help any company see their way through chaotic events. He has taught these principles at Carnegie Melon University where he has been on the faculty or teaching staff for over 30 years.

Index

OTHER TITLES IN THE HUMAN RESOURCE MANAGEMENT AND ORGANIZATIONAL BEHAVIOR COLLECTION

Michael J. Provitera and Michael Edmondson, Editors

- *Nice Guys Finish Last And Other Workplace Lies,* by John Ruffa
- *Understanding and Using AI* by Daniel O. Livvarcin and Yacouba Traoré
- *The Leadership Edge* by Michael B. Ross and Mike Shaw
- *Business and Management in the Age of Intangible Capitalism* by Hamid Yeganeh
- *Ignite All* by The Fusion Team
- *(Re)Value* by Adam Wallace and Adam Wallace
- *Dysfunctional Organizations* by David D. Van Fleet
- *The Negotiation Edge* by Michael Saksa
- *Applied Leadership* by Sam Altawil
- *Forging Dynasty Businesses* by Chuck Violand
- *How the Harvard Business School Changed the Way We View Organizations* by Jay W. Lorsch
- *Managing Millennials* by Jacqueline Cripps
- *Personal Effectiveness* by Lucia Strazzeri
- *Catalyzing Transformation* by Sandra Waddock
- *Nurturing Equanimity* by Michael Edmondson

Concise and Applied Business Books

The Collection listed above is one of 30 business subject collections that Business Expert Press has grown to make BEP a premiere publisher of print and digital books. Our concise and applied books are for…

- Professionals and Practitioners
- Faculty who adopt our books for courses
- Librarians who know that BEP's Digital Libraries are a unique way to offer students ebooks to download, not restricted with any digital rights management
- Executive Training Course Leaders
- Business Seminar Organizers

Business Expert Press books are for anyone who needs to dig deeper on business ideas, goals, and solutions to everyday problems. Whether one print book, one ebook, or buying a digital library of 110 ebooks, we remain the affordable and smart way to be business smart. For more information, please visit www.businessexpertpress.com, or contact sales@businessexpertpress.com.